C0-AVH-136

A Cybernetic Approach to
the Assessment of Children

Other Titles of Interest

The Psychology and Education of Gifted Children, Philip Vernon, Georgina Adamson, and Dorothy Vernon

The Danish National Child Care System: A Successful System as Model for the Reconstruction of American Child Care, Marsden Wagner and Mary Wagner

Found: Long-Term Gains From Early Intervention, Bernard Brown

Beyond Surface Curriculum: An Interview Study of Teachers' Understandings, Anne M. Bussis, Edward Chittenden, and Marianne Amarel

A Westview Special Study

*A Cybernetic Approach to
the Assessment of Children:
Toward a More Humane Use
of Human Beings*
edited by Mark N. Ozer

This collection addresses the application of the principles of cybernetics to the methodology of assessment of function in children. The authors suggest that an awareness of the issues of control and informational feedback exemplified by cybernetics leads to new ways of thinking about both the process of gathering data and the type of data sought. Without attempting to reach a total consensus or to impart the sense of a fully developed system, they apply a new paradigm that may lead to greater recognition of the inherent individuality of human beings and provide the scientific basis of a more humane approach to assessment.

Mark N. Ozer is associate professor of child health and development at the George Washington University School of Medicine. In his private practice he treats children with developmental problems and a wide range of neurological diseases.

A Cybernetic Approach to the Assessment of Children: Toward a More Humane Use of Human Beings

edited by Mark N. Ozer

Westview Press / Boulder, Colorado

0349????

107294

A Westview Special Study

All rights reserved. No part of this publication may be reproduced or transmitted in any form or by any means, electronic or mechanical, including photocopy, recording, or any information storage and retrieval system, without permission in writing from the publisher.

Copyright © 1979 by Westview Press, Inc.

Published in 1979 in the United States of America by

Westview Press, Inc.
5500 Central Avenue
Boulder, Colorado 80301
Frederick A. Praeger, Publisher

Library of Congress Cataloging in Publication Data
Main entry under title:
A Cybernetic approach to the assessment of children.
    (A Westview special study)
    Includes bibliographical references.
    1. Psychological tests for children. 2. Information theory in psychology.
I. Ozer, Mark N.
BF722.C9   155.4'028   79-12872
ISBN 0-89158-466-8

Printed and bound in the United States of America

*To my father: whose life
has been devoted to the search for
more humane relationships between human beings.*

Contents

ix

0349558
107294

PART 3
THE APPLICATION OF CYBERNETICS TO THE
ASSESSMENT OF CHILDREN

1
Introduction

Mark N. Ozer

This volume is an outgrowth of a symposium, titled "Toward the Human Use of Human Beings: A Cybernetic Approach to the Assessment of Children," delivered at the February 1977 meeting of the American Association for the Advancement of Science in Denver. Sponsored by the American Society for Cybernetics and the Psychology, Education, and Information Sciences section of the AAAS, the symposium met with considerable enthusiasm as an interdisciplinary attempt to apply the principles of cybernetics, the science of control and communication, to certain issues of child development. Some of the papers contained in this volume are amplifications of addresses given at that meeting, and others represent the contributions of scientists whose work could not be encompassed within the time limits imposed by the symposium format.

The book applies to the assessment of children the promise of cybernetics, originally defined by Norbert Wiener in his book *The Human Use of Human Beings*. First published in the era of the Cold War in 1950, Wiener's book was described by Walter Rosenblith, in the Afterword of its revised edition in 1964, as an attempt to stimulate discussion of the social implications of the "cybernetic revolution." Rosenblith went on to emphasize the purpose of the book in terms of the moral imperative suggested by its title.

Wiener's subtitle, *Cybernetics and Society*, conveyed its

1

intent to outline some visions for the future. A sense of hope for the future, somewhat subdued by the climate of political repression in which the book was conceived, may be illustrated by the following quotation from its Preface.

> While the universe as a whole . . . tends to run down, there are local enclaves whose direction seems opposed to that of the universe at large and in which there is a limited and temporary tendency for organization to increase. Life finds its home in some of these enclaves. It is with this point of view at its core that the new science of Cybernetics began its development. . . . The existence of these islands enables some of us to assert the existence of progress.

Wiener went on to explore the social implications of the physiological substrate of humans as distinguished from that of the more fixed social organizations of other animals.

> Variety and possibility are inherent in the human sensorium and are indeed the key to man's most noble flights because variety and possibility belong to the very structure of the human organism. . . . The human species is strong only insofar as it takes advantage of the innate, adaptive learning faculties that its physiological structure makes possible.

The application of the principle of feedback, although it first arose in the design of machines, does not lead to the mechanization of people, Wiener pointed out. Rather, the awareness of the variety inherent in the human coupled with the concept of feedback permits a more effective means by which freedom may be achieved.

> Feedback is a method of controlling a system by inserting into it the results of its past performance. If these results are merely used as numerical data for the criticism of the system and its regulation, we have the simple feedback of the control engineers. If, however, the information which proceeds backward from the performance is able to change the general method and pattern of performance, we have a process which may well be called learning. . . . [One] must be able to record whether the general plan . . . has been on the whole successful or not, and . . . must be able

to change the plan. . . . This form of learning is most certainly a feedback but it is a feedback of a higher level, a feedback of policies and not of simple actions.

Wiener saw this potential for higher-level regulation as the principal contribution of cybernetics to human development.

Coincident with th development of the concept of feedback was its application to the elucidation of central nervous system function. Wiener described, in his Introduction to the original edition of *Cybernetics* in 1948, the fruitful interdisciplinary interchange in which the concept of feedback arose during the Second World War. The explanation of the existence of ataxia (loss of motor coordination) in the human could be more clearly stated in terms of abnormalities in the degree of feedback in the nervous system. Ataxia may be due to *insufficient* sensory feedback secondary to destruction of sensory pathways in the spinal cord or due to *increased* feedback secondary to disease of the cerebellar centers for the modulation of motor function. Herein was some confirmation of feedback as a general phenomenon, and the implications of this concept led to a new model of the nervous system.

> The central nervous system no longer appears as a self-contained organ, receiving inputs from the senses and discharging into the muscles. On the contrary, some of its most characteristic activities are explicable only as circular processes, emerging from the nervous system into the muscles, and re-entering the nervous system through the sense organs, whether they be proprioceptors or the organs of the special senses. . . . The performance of the nervous system [was] as an integrated whole.

The neurophysiologist Warren McCulloch provided me with the link between the ideas first expressed by Wiener and those contained in the present volume. I had the good fortune to meet him in 1967 when, as a neurologist, I was concerned with the development of more effective and humane techniques for the assessment of brain function in children and adults with learning problems. With encouragement from McCulloch and others, my work has proceeded since.

This volume focuses on the principles of cybernetics as they might be applied to human systems. In 1971 Heinz von Foerster staked out the areas of our enquiry when he divided the concerns of cybernetics into the "single brain" problem, or the brain sciences, and the "two-brain" problem of education. It is this latter area of enquiry that this volume more specifically addresses. Von Foerster stated the problem as follows:

> It is clear that the majority of our established educational efforts is directed toward the trivialization of our children. I use the term "trivialization" exactly as used in automata theory, where a "trivial" machine is characterized by its fixed input-output relation, while in a "non-trivial" machine the output is determined by the input *and* its internal state. Since our educational system is geared to generate predictable citizens, its aim is to amputate the bothersome internal states which generate unpredictability and novelty. This is most clearly demonstrated by our method of examination in which only questions are asked for which the answers are known (or defined), and are to be memorized by the student. I shall call these questions "illegitimate questions." Would it not be fascinating to think of an educational system that de-trivializes its students by teaching them to ask "legitimate questions," that is, questions for which the answers are unknown?

The science of control and communication applied to such problems requires, in my opinion, an increase in the *sharing* of control and communication in the developmental sequence in children. It is the growth of the child's ability to be aware of his own self-regulating role that is the measure of development. The sharing by the adult of such awareness in a dialogue in which "legitimate" questions are asked of the child contributes to his capability to do the same.

The assessment or examination procedures to evaluate this development are the topic of this volume. The traditional assessment process has viewed the person being examined as subject to the examiner. The application of a cybernetic approach offers a model for the revision of the power relationship that has direct relevance to child development. To examine the process of child development, this volume argues, the examiner should simulate it. He must bring about the process in the very activity of sampling it, must stimulate it during the short time span of any examination. The individual being examined is part of an interaction and must become aware of some reciprocal effect upon the other as a simulation of what actually happens in the process of growth and development. Even with rather young children, it becomes possible to make such reciprocal effects explicit by providing feedback of the input provided by each to the interaction. It is the evidence of reciprocity of the interaction made explicit by such feedback that is the crucial parameter distinguishing the human use of cybernetic concepts.

It is felt that the awareness of control and informational feedback incorporated in the definition of cybernetics will lead to new ways of considering both the process of gathering data about children and the type of data that is sought. It is suggested that the useful data may well be those of the process by which the child learns. This is, I suggest, a "legitimate" question in von Foerster's terms for which the answers are unknown. These answers can never be known by another without the contributions by the person who is doing the learning. These are data not only for the examiner but, even more important, for the person being examined.

Lack of awareness of the interactive character of the assessment process has limited the usefulness of the information obtained by existing methods. The rigor offered by cybernetics provides a scientific basis for a revolution in the fields of psychology and child development consistent with the findings of Piaget as well as others. Conversely, this mode of thinking offers a way to reconceptualize the process of development that leads to greater recognition of the inherent individuality of human beings. It provides a scientific basis for a more humane approach to assessment and to education.

This volume is intended mainly for graduate students and practitioners in the fields of education, child development, human development, and psychology. The emphasis is on some of the issues of assessment from a cybernetic viewpoint —but this is not a textbook on cybernetics or on assessment.

It is designed to open the mind of the student and practitioner to the implications of such an approach. The chapters
are therefore in the form of essays on various aspects of
assessment, drawn from the experiences of the various
authors, without extensive references. Each chapter may be
read as complete within itself, but the flow of the book is
also important; some of the earlier material constitutes
background for the later chapters on application of the principles.

The first section of the book therefore provides some of
the theoretical substrate for the later chapters. The first
chapter by William Powers provides an introduction to cybernetics, to the principle of the control of perception, and to a
hierarchical model for such control systems. The second
chapter by Ernst von Glasersfeld completes the more theoretical section with emphasis on the inter-relationship of the
concepts of cybernetics and those of Piaget.

The chapter by Hugh Petrie marks the transition to the
issue of assessment and the introduction to the second main
section. His chapter on the issue of subjective and objective
tests is followed and complemented by Howard Gallas and
Irving Sigel's on the research in assessing child development.
His thesis is that the *"méthode clinique"* of Piaget is an
example of the interactive assessment mode.

The third major section concerns the actual application of
interactive methods of assessment both in research settings
and in educational practice. The chapter by Rod Cocking
explores the value of a more interactive assessment in the
measurement of language in young children, and the last
chapter, by Mark Ozer, applies the principles of cybernetics
to the entire system for assessment of children with learning
problems. In this final section, the emphasis is on the practical application of the principles introduced in the first
section and made more specific as to testing and examination
procedures in the second section.

In closing this introduction, one may perhaps once again
refer to the book by Wiener that provided some of the inspira-
tion for the focus of the present volume. In his 1950 book, *The
Human Use of Human Beings,* he said that part of the pur-

pose of cybernetics is "to develop a language and techniques that will enable us to attack the problem of control and communication in general, but also to find the proper repertory of ideas and techniques to classify their particular manifestations under those certain concepts." This volume, a generation later, marks at least in some small part a realization of the particular manifestations specific to the measurement of brain function in children under the guidance of the basic concepts of cybernetics.

References

McCulloch, W. S. 1965. *The Embodiments of Mind.* Cambridge, Mass.: M.I.T. Press.

von Foerster, H. 1971. The responsibility of competence. *Cybernetics Technique in Brain Research and the Educational Process.* Washington, D.C.: American Society for Cybernetics.

Wiener, N. 1948. *Cybernetics.* Cambridge, Mass.: M.I.T. Press.

Wiener, N. 1950. *The Human Use of Human Beings.* Boston, Mass.: Houghton Mifflin.

Part 1

Cybernetic Theory: Research
Models in Child Development

2

A Cybernetic Model for Research in Human Development

William T. Powers

Over the past thirty years, cybernetics has gone in many directions. It is sometimes difficult to see how some modern approaches that go under that name relate to the original concept proposed by Norbert Wiener (1948): the concept that organisms display the characteristics of negative feedback control systems. Since this concept represented the chief revolutionary departure of cybernetics from conventional thinking, one might expect every person claiming to be a cyberneticist to understand the principles of control theory, at least at the level of valid rules of thumb. This is not the case. What most "cyberneticians" do and write is perfectly compatible with traditional models of organisms, and hence is incompatible with the principles of control theory. In this volume, we hope to improve on that state of affairs.

The original promise of a cybernetic revolution in our understanding of human nature can still, I am confident, be realized. To bring it about, however, we must be prepared to change some concepts that have been defended for a long time. We must also be prepared to return for a while to a relatively low level of abstraction, so as to grasp the meaning of control theory in relationship to simple direct experiences. The first step in launching a cybernetic revolution in psychology is to make sure that the fundamental phenomena of control are correctly understood in relationship to behavior.

In this chapter I will be presenting a primer in control theory for behavioral scientists. While this book is concerned with human development, I think most readers would agree that research concerning *how* human beings develop into adults must be strongly conditioned by *what* one considers to be the nature of an adult organization. A thorough grasp of the principles of control systems will provide a picture of development considerably different from what one would obtain from, say, Freudian theory or behaviorism. Near the end, I will take a few steps toward applying this theory specifically to development, but only as any theoretician points out general directions to experimentalists or clinicians.

Background

Controlling various aspects of experience is an activity that has engaged human beings throughout recorded history. Until the middle 1930s, however, no human being was able to say, in a systematic and quantitative way, just what the term "control" meant. Like digestion, control was a natural process of which we could take advantage without any understanding of how it works.

Otto Mayr's book, *The Origins of Feedback Control* (1970), is a history of all known control devices from the water-level regulator of Ktsebios in the third century B.C. to the automatic watch regulator of Bregeut near the beginning of the nineteenth century. It is a slim volume. It shows that control systems were, during this 2,100-year period, freaks in a world of "normal" machines designed according to completely different principles. Control devices were built, but control principles were unknown; there was no development of a body of knowledge that could be passed along the generations. The concept of mechanism that developed at the time of the Renaissance and led to the first Industrial Revolution was based on a particular concept of cause and effect, in which one set of circumstances led through rigid linkages to the next, in strict temporal and spatial sequence. This concept of mechanism lay at the foundations of all the new sciences: physics, chemistry, and biology. No scientist, no engineer, realized that in the control system a different arrangement of cause and effect existed.

In 1868, James Clerk Maxwell (1965) published the differential equations for Watt's flyball governor. By using differential equations, Maxwell employed a method that transcends simple cause and effect for two reasons. First, the variables used in differential equations involve time-derivatives, and in the solutions, time integrals, representations involving processes that span time. The solutions of a set of differential equations arise from causes occurring not at an instant, but over an interval. Second, the equations Maxwell used dealt with processes in a *closed loop*. By breaking the governor down into part-systems, representing each part by an equation, and then solving the equations as a simultaneous system, Maxwell effectively removed temporal sequence from the picture and substituted simultaneous interactions in a circle with no beginning and no end.

This development occurred just as experimental psychology was becoming a science in Germany. It led to a long chain of developments—but in mechanics, not in psychology. The implicit new concept of mechanism remained implicit, being unrecognized even by engineers. Psychology continued to employ the old concept of mechanism, so that when the American psychologist James Watson announced the birth of behaviorism just after the turn of the twentieth century, he rested his case, as biology had done before him, on the assertion that such mechanisms as Maxwell had analyzed could exist only in a metaphysician's imagination.

As far as Watson was concerned, and as far as any life scientists of his time were concerned, organisms could obey the laws of nature only in one way. They must be basically passive devices set into motion by external forces. However intricate their inner construction, they could do nothing of themselves. Aquinas, trying to prove the existence of God, had declared that nothing moves of itself. Those in the life sciences who were trying to prove the opposite said the same thing.

In reaction against the idea that the universe worked according to the whims of Divine Purpose instead of discoverable

Natural Law, life scientists have always made the mistake of assuming that purpose is a metaphysical fancy. This prejudice prevented them from looking into the many instances of behavior in which purpose appeared obvious; rather than asking what kind of organization could select its own goals and act so as to achieve them, the great majority of life scientists agreed that this appearance must be an illusion. They set themselves the task, at least tacitly, of dispelling the illusion by constructing cause-effect explanations in which physics and chemistry alone lay at the base, and external events worked through known physical processes to produce the apparently purposeful behavior. This, of course, left subjective phenomena in the role of accidental side-effects, and removed from organisms all capability for directing their own actions.

This logical scheme entered psychology as the twentieth century began, but its roots were in biology, medicine, physics, and chemistry. There is, therefore, a tremendous weight of tradition behind it. Whole disciplines are founded on it. Knowledge built on knowledge is also built on the assumption, which we can now prove false, that organisms cannot have internal purposes. Removal of that assumption will have profound and, from one point of view, disastrous effects.

Control theory finally became a formal system during World War II. By that time engineers had succeeded in building devices that imitated the human ability to act on the outside world and to control numerous aspects of it, and had found the mathematics for analyzing and designing such systems. Many of them were aware of the similarities of control system behavior to that of living systems. Norbert Wiener and his neurologist friend Rosenbleuth may have thought they were discoverers of this parallel, but I suspect that their engineer-collaborator, Bigelow, had been aware of it for a longer time. Engineers, after all, were the ones who gave such names as sensor and comparator to parts of control systems and whose job it was to analyze human tasks for the purpose of designing machines that could take them over.

I think there is also evidence that neither engineers nor the new cyberneticists realized that control theory entailed a concept of mechanism that went beyond the concepts at the foundations of the life sciences. Most engineers are dyed-in-the-wool mechanists, trained in the same ideas of cause and effect that have always been accepted. In a famous debate (Buckley, 1968), Wiener did not make the crucial distinctions between a passive, nonpurposive system (a compass) and an active, purposive system (a homing missile). They could not throw off the old point of view sufficiently to see that they were themselves talking about a new one.

Thirty years have gone by since Wiener joined a scientific revolution and coined a name for it. The confusion may finally be clearing up, the false trails may be in the process of abandonment. What we have left is considerably simpler than what cybernetics has gone through in those decades, but it is also fundamental. The message that Wiener gave us is not as complex as he made it out to be, and it is more important than he realized when he gave it. Organisms are purposive. Purpose is not a metaphysical concept. Behavior is a link in a process by which organisms control the most important effects that the environment has on them.

Let us turn now to Psychology 101 (ca. 1988). We begin by looking at ordinary behavior to see how control phenomena appear to an observer. Then we look at an elementary model of organization that can account, at least in terms of one real possibility, for what is observed. After that, I will present a picture of possible levels of organization in a human hierarchy of control organizations, and at the end, at last, some remarks of how this whole approach might be applied to research in human development. Anyone writing at the early stages of a scientific revolution has to rely on reason and supposition more than on hard data, but I can trust that the readers of this volume will be able to distinguish well-founded principles from conjectures about their application.

Characteristics of a Control System

The Phenomenon of Control

Control phenomena can be found in any example of

TABLE 1

Control actions involved in getting
ready to back a stick-shift car out
of a driveway.

Behavior	Means	Variable	Reference state
Open door	Grasp, pull	Angle of door	80 degrees
Get in	Bend, sit, slide	Relationship to seat.	Seated
Shut door	Grasp, pull	Angle of door	0 degrees
Fasten belt	Push together	distance between fasteners	Zero distance
Adjust rear view mirror	Grasp, twist	Displacement, rear window image	Zero displacement
Depress clutch	Push with left leg	Extension of leg	Fully extended
Insert key	Extend arm	Distance, key to keyhole	Zero distance
Start engine	Twist	Sound of starter and engine	Whirrrrrr, vroom!
Shift to reverse	Grasp, push	Position of shift lever	Coordinates of reverse gear

behavior, even the briefest snapshot of ordinary activities. Consider an episode that lasts perhaps thirty seconds. A man gets in his car, starts the engine, puts the car in gear, and backs out of the driveway. Table 1 is a partial listing of activities that are likely to occur during this brief event. Each activity involves four items, the first of which is in the Behavior column. In this column are phrases of a kind used both in ordinary discourse and in scientific psychology to denote what an organism is doing. Even though Watson (1919) wrote that behaviorists, when necessary, reduce any behavior described at this level to a collection of individual reflex movements, he never actually did so. Nor has anyone else since. This is the level at which most scientists perceive the actions of organisms. No analysis takes place: instead, instances of behaviors described this way are counted, and the sums are used in statistical manipulations. We will at least try to analyze, but not with the results anticipated by Watson.

Consider the first item: Open Door. The meaning is obvious. The door which was shut becomes open, and the driver did it.

The problem here, as in so many areas of psychology, lies in unspoken assumptions and relationships taken for granted. The opening of the door is certainly an event, but this event can be produced in innumerable ways. The door is not part of the driver. It is an object that can be in a number of states, and its state is determined by the sum of all forces that act on it. To say that the door opens says nothing about the driver.

The opening of the door tells us only that sufficient force existed to make the door swing open. There are many forces normally acting on a car door. Any tilt of the car is translated, owing to gravity, into a force tending to open or close the door. If a wind is blowing, it too exerts forces on the door. The door is held fully open by a mechanical detent, which resists the effects of other forces up to a point. While the door is moving, friction in its hinges and inertial effects of its mass create more forces. All these effects are normally present no matter how the door is being opened.

To say that the driver opens the door means only that the driver adds forces of his own to others that are acting on the door at the same time. He does not open the door by means of opening the door. He does it by *grasping* the handle, and by *pulling* on it. The second column of Table 1 lists some of the means used by the driver in bringing about each "behavior." We can see immediately that the real actions of the driver—the effects which we can attribute to the driver alone—are all in the Means column. What is so casually called behavior results from the conjunction of many forces, only one of which is contributed by the driver. The Behavior column really lists *consequences* of the driver's actions, consequences that are not determined by the driver's actions, but are only influenced by them.

By paying careful, even compulsive, attention to detail, we have uncovered a problem. What is casually called behavior, the opening of the door, is not something that could be attributed to the driver's actions alone. It results from the conjunction of many effects, only one of which is contributed by the driver. This problem exists for every entry in the Behavior column, and in fact for nearly any kind of behavior that can be mentioned, for any organism from the bacterium to the human being. "Behavior" is really a consequence that results from adding together many influences, the majority of which act even in the absence of the behaving organism. To speak this loosely of behavior, therefore, is to gloss over a fundamental problem that must be solved before any theory of behavior can possibly make sense.

Instead of standing back and noting that in a fuzzy sort of way the driver's action "opens the door," let us continue to pay attention to detail, asking *how* this behavior unfolds. The phrase "opens the door" refers to an amalgam of ongoing processes, mixed with implications about starting and ending conditions; it is sloppy, as most ordinary language is. In ordinary discourse, we can often straighten out the message as we receive it, but in science that sort of informality is worse than useless.

The driver's action, combined with other forces, does not simply conjure up an event out of nothing. It produces a process that goes smoothly from a starting condition to a final condition. At every moment during this process, there is a *variable*, the angle made by the door and the car frame, that has some particular value and some rate of change. This variable, and not "the door," is what changes, what is influenced by all the forces being applied. (Column 3 of Table 1 is a listing of some of the variables associated with each behavior.) We can represent the bulk of what is meant by opening the door in terms of the way this variable changes from one value (0 degrees) to another (say, 80 degrees), going through all the intermediate angles.

The driver will pull on the door hard enough to overcome the resistance of the door, counteract wind and gravity forces, and start the door swinging open. He will stop pulling when the door is open, meaning that the angle has become 80 degrees. We can confidently expect that this will occur no matter what the wind or the tilt of the car, and no matter what car is involved. It does not matter that on one occasion the driver may have to pull with a force of 1 pound and on the next (with a different car, wind, and tilt) a force of 50 pounds. The driver will simply pull *hard enough* to produce the result we expect.

So by being patient we have uncovered a second major problem. What is uniform about this behavior (or any of the behaviors listed) is that it occurs regardless of even large variations in extraneous factors that contribute to the final result. The action in the Means column changes from one occasion to the next in just the way needed to make up for changes in other contributions. The variations in action are not small; if the wind blows hard enough to propel the door by itself, the driver might open the door by *pushing* (after it is partly open).

Column 4 of Table 1, Reference State, refers to the final condition to which the variable is brought despite any ordinary disturbance. The existence of these reference states is not conjectural; once behavior has been defined in terms of an appropriate variable, such reference states always exist. They can be discovered experimentally, and defined in terms of observable relationships. Whether or not they *should* exist according to anyone's theory, they *do* exist.

In these reference states we have the heart of the problem to which control theory is addressed. What kind of system can behave in such a way that a variable will, under a variety of unpredictable conditions, always approach the same state? What determines that state? *Where* is that state determined— that is, by what? To dismiss the existence of reference states as an illusion is simply to discard data. To explain such reference states as the inevitable outcome of prior causes in the outside world is to demand experimental verification of a kind that has never been found. To say that "subtle cues," which are so subtle as to escape the notice of a careful observer, cause the singularly appropriate variations of action is to abandon science.

Reference states cannot exist under the old cause-effect model. They refer, as far as external observations are concerned, only to future states of the organism or its environment. They cannot affect present behavior, and they must be treated simply as *outcomes* of events caused by prior events. The flaw in this reasoning is hard to see if one does not know (as the founders of scientific psychology did not know) of organizations capable of complex internal activities that are essentially independent of current external events. By ruling out the possibility of significant causes of behavior *inside* the organism, where they could not be observed, early behavioral scientists in effect committed themselves to a whole chain of deductions following from the assumption that everything of significance with regard to behavior could be observed from outside the organism. They were betting everything on the assumption that such internal causes would never be found to exist, partly because the methods they used could not be valid if such inner causes *did* exist. So when we speak of reference states here, we are resurrecting a corpse that was buried a long time ago and which is still preferred by many to be left underground. Only control theory justifies this disinterment.

There is one explanation for the existence of reference states that has been proposed over and over for centuries: they are determined by the *intentions* of the behaving organism. The driver has, inside him, the intention that the door be open. He acts to achieve this purpose, doing whatever is required (if possible) to achieve it. This simple and parsimonious explanation has only one fault, or had prior to control theory: intentions are "mental" phenomena, and here we are asking them to have "physical" effects. This apparent difficulty has stopped scientific psychology in its tracks for some 75 years if not more.

There is another approach to the problem. Instead of automatically assuming that mental and physical phenomena have nothing to do with each other, we can assume that there is no contradiction and try to find out how this result is brought about—how the phenomenon of inner purpose or intention works. We do not have to accept the idea that the future can affect the present, nor do we have to repudiate any useful principles of physics and chemistry that have been so carefully constructed. All we have to do is find an organization that can do what we observe being done. That is what we shall now do.

The Organization of a Control System

For *any* of the "variables" of Table 1 to be brought to specific reference states, the driver must be able to sense them—either directly, or by sensing something that covaries with the variable we choose to measure the behavior. Elementary experiments would be enough to establish this principle. If the driver had to execute any of the behaviors in Table 1 blindly, with no visual, auditory, kinesthetic, or other sensory information to tell him the current status of the variable, it would be impossible for him to vary his actions so as to oppose unexpected disturbances. In fact, we would find through continuing experiment that the only reliable consequences of the driver's actions are those the driver can sense. This is a crucial hint about how this sort of phenomenon is created.

It is necessary for the driver to sense the controlled variable, but not sufficient. Suppose the dirver senses the position of the gearshift lever. He senses the position known as first gear. Does this imply *pull* or does it imply *push?* By itself, the information given by the position of the shift lever does not imply *any* action. It merely indicates the current state of affairs. The driver needs to know where the lever *is to be,* not just where it is.

By the same token, it is not sufficient for the driver to know where the lever *is to be*. If the lever is to be in the neutral position, the action required to put it there depends on where the lever *is*. No amount of description of the reference condition can, by itself, lead to an action that will make the controlled variable approach it.

Creating an action which will bring the controlled variable to some specific reference condition depends on information contained partly in the present state of the variable and partly in some specification of its reference condition. The direction and amount of action that is required depends on the direction and amount of discrepancy between these two quantities. Therefore, in order for this discrepancy to be corrected reliably, the driver must be organized to detect its amount and direction and to convert it into those coordinated acts that will systematically reduce the discrepancy. A decreasing discrepancy should lead to a decreasing amount of action, and a reversal of the discrepancy should lead to a reversal of the action. A change in direction of the discrepancy should produce a corresponding change in direction of the action, so the action is always aimed against the direction of the discrepancy.

We have, therefore, what amounts to a design problem. It is instructive to see how the engineers of the 1930s solved it, being unaware that purposes or goals were metaphysical constructs.

Suppose an angular position like that of the car door is to be controlled. The first step is to provide a means of *sensing* it. To the engineer, this means converting the angle of the door into something with which an electronic circuit can deal, say a voltage. This can be done easily by attaching a transducer to the door hinge, a transducer that generates an output of 80 volts when the angle is 80 degrees and 0 volts when the angle is 0 degrees, and that varies between these voltages as the door varies its position between those angular limits. This sort of representation is known as *analog* representation. The signal generated by the transducer does not change position or angle as the door does, but each *magnitude* of the signal corresponds to one *position* of the door.

The same system would work in a brain. As the image of the car door on the driver's retina changes, and as other kinds of information change, some signal in the driver's brain varies in magnitude in a corresponding way. Magnitudes in a neurological model correspond to frequencies of firing. Of course more than simple sensing is required; the uncountable signals from many kinds of sensory receptors must be combined through real-time neural computations to generate a position signal like that from the transducer.

The transducer signal merely indicates where the door is, not where it is to be. Since the position of the door now exists as a voltage analog, a particular position corresponds to a particular voltage. It is easy to arrange for a second source of voltage, independent of the transducer, which can be set to create any voltage between 0 and 80 volts. This voltage would be called the *reference signal.* If the reference signal were set to 65 volts, then if the transducer signal were somehow made to match it, we could deduce that the door must stand at an angle of 65 degrees. Thus setting the reference signal to some specific voltage is equivalent to specifying some particular state of the variable that is being sensed—the angle of the car door.

If we can imagine a neural signal that is the brain's analog of the car door angle, it is certainly easy to imagine another neural signal, independent of the sensory signals affected by the position of the door, which is fixed in magnitude between the magnitude limits of the sense-derived signal. If, somehow, the sensory signal could be made to match the neural reference signal in magnitude, the angle of the door would be indirectly specified by the setting of the reference signal.

In the electronic control system it is a simple matter to subtract one signal from another, leaving a difference signal. This is done with an electronic *subtractor,* or, as it is known in control applications, a *comparator.* This is a device which responds only to the algebraic (signed) difference between two voltages and generates an output voltage whose magnitude depends on the magnitude of the difference, the sign depending on the sign of the difference (voltages can be either positive or negative). This output of a comparator is called by engineers an *error signal.*

Subtraction can also be accomplished with neurones. If two neural signals combine at one nerve cell, one may act to excite firings of that cell while the other acts to inhibit firings of that cell. Both excitation and inhibition take place in a smooth, graded manner, provided one treats the phenomena in terms of frequencies of firing and neurotransmitter concentrations, not single impulses. The frequency with which the receiving cell fires then depends on the *difference* in frequencies between an exciting and an inhibiting input. Frequencies cannot go negative, but if a second cell existed in which the roles of excitation and inhibition by the two incoming signals were interchanged, the two cells together could generate a pair of error signals, one representing "too large" and the other representing "too small." Absence of both signals would mean that the sensory input signal exactly matches the reference input signal.

To complete the artificial car door control system, the engineer needs only to convert the electronic error voltage into an effect on the car door. A positive voltage should act to increase the angle, a negative voltage to decrease it. This is accomplished by letting the error voltage enter a power amplifier, which boosts the level of energy from that of an information-carrying signal to that of a power source capable of running a motor, still retaining the basic directionality and magnitude information in the error signal. If a positive voltage means that the transducer signal is less than the reference signal and turns the motor to *open* the door, and if a negative voltage means the opposite and causes the opposite direction of turning of the motor, the door will be urged toward a reference state whether it is initially too far open or too far shut.

It is the same in the brain. If the pair of error signals is converted either into a push or a pull depending on the sign of the error (i.e., which of the pair of error signals is present), and if the magnitude of the effort depends on the magnitude of the error, the car door will always be urged toward the position in which it would generate a sensory

107294

signal equal to the reference signal.

The engineers who devised systems that could imitate human control behavior proved, by the expedient of building examples of their model, that this model of human organization does in fact work. Of course many other organizations would also work, since there are many ways to sense an angle, and many more complex ways of converting an error into an action that will correct an angle error. But all such alternate systems are equivalent to the organization we have just been through, and none of them is equivalent to the simple cause-effect model that tradition assumes. Thus the existence of working artificial control systems supplies us with an existence theorem, proving that a real physical system can act to make a variable approach a preselected state with no metaphysical assumptions at all being needed. Given that proof, we do not have to worry about whether the model we adopt is exactly the correct one or not. We know we have the right *kind* of model and can commence finding the correct one of that kind through the usual scientific procedures of hypothesis-testing.

Perhaps now the difference between the old cause-effect linear model and the control-system model is becoming more apparent. Under the old model, stimuli were thought to act on the nervous system to cause muscle tensions; those muscle tensions caused the limbs to move, and those motions in turn created all the effects we call behavior. It was assumed that the final patterns were simply the sums of all the detailed muscle tensions, added according to the laws of vector addition and creating consequences according to the laws of mechanics. If disturbances entered in such a way as to cause changes between the time of the generation of muscle tensions and the later consequences of those tensions, one could not predict logically that the consequences would remain the same.

Control theory predicts that the consequences—or at least certain of them—*will* remain the same despite such disturbances. They will remain the same because the organism is sensing them and varying its actions to maintain those consequences in relation to specific reference states. As disturbances vary their effects on the ultimate consequence, the organism varies its own effects in just the way that will cancel the effects of the disturbance. Since the consequence itself is being monitored, the source of the disturbance makes no difference and need not be sensed. (Sensing the cause of a disturbance creates "feed-forward," which is sometimes useful, but never essential.)

In brief, the old model says that organisms are organized to produced predetermined *actions.* Control theory says that organisms are organized to produce internally selected *perceptions,* which in many cases are perceptions of the same events that the external observer sees as the organism's behavior. The organism acts to bring under control, in relation to some reference state, the sensed perceptions.

The Properties of a Control System

The concept of control behavior as a process of error correction is helpful as a way to understand the general organization of control systems but is misleading with respect to most interesting kinds of control behavior. Given only what we have seen above, one might think that the brain selects or generates a reference signal, and that behavior is then produced by a control system that gradually brings its sensory signal to a match with the reference signal. There may be cases of complex and time-consuming actions that should be seen in this way, but I rather doubt it, and I will try to explain why.

Let's consider a case in which the driver might open the car door *part-way,* for instance, while backing out of the driveway and looking out the door. This action involves setting a reference-position for the door that is between 0 and 80 degrees, and *maintaining* the door in that position despite tilts of the car and gusts of wind.

To understand what *maintaining* implies, we begin with the door at its reference position, say 30 degrees. In this position, the door generates a sensory analog that exactly matches a reference signal generated elsewhere in the driver's brain.

If the door were actually at exactly that position, there

would clearly be no error signal in the driver's brain. If there were no error signal, the driver's muscle systems would be driven neither to pull nor to push. If any disturbance then arose, there would be nothing to oppose its tendency to move the door, and the door would begin to swing to angles higher or lower than 30 degrees.

Suppose a disturbance swings the door more open. As the angle reaches 31 degrees, 1 degree of error appears. Suppose that for each degree of error, 100 grams of pull are generated by the muscles. Suppose further that the disturbance causing this error is equivalent to a force of 5 kilograms (5,000 grams) acting at the same place the driver's hand acts, but to open the door. We can see immediately that the door will continue to open until the error is large enough to produce 5,000 grams of pull by the muscles that will cancel the disturbing force and prevent any further opening. (We are neglecting inertial effects here.) How far beyond the reference position does the door have to be to generate a pull by the driver amounting to 5,000 grams? Fifty degrees, since each degree generates 100 grams of pull. The door will end up at an angle of 80 degrees, fully open.

The driver's *error sensitivity*, we can say, is 100 grams of effort per degree of error. Let us now suppose that this error sensitivity becomes 10 times as large, or 1,000 grams per degree. How far will the door now depart from its reference condition under a disturbance of 5,000 grams? Five degrees. It will swing to an angle of 30 + 5, or 35 degrees. A disturbance of the same size but tending to *close* the door would generate the opposite sense of error, producing a push; if the push error sensitivity were also 1,000 grams per degree (it need not be the same as the pull sensitivity), the door would swing to 25 degrees, 5 degrees less than the reference setting.

Continuing in this vein, if the error sensitivity becomes 10,000 grams per degree, a 5,000-gram disturbance would move the door only 0.5 degree form its reference position: at 100,000 grams per degree, the error would be only 0.05 degree. The higher the error sensitivity, the stiffer this control system would seem to another person pushing on the door—the less it would yield to a push.

If we say that an error of 1 degree is small enough to be unimportant with regard to any of the driver's purposes, it clearly ceases to matter what his error sensitivity is as long as it is greater than 5,000 grams per degree (and disturbances remain less than 5,000 grams). Furthermore, if the man's error sensitivity is 10 times that required minimum, there will be essentially no effect on the controlled variable if his error sensitivity *changes*—if it increases by any amount, or decreases by any factor smaller than 10. If the driver were required to hold the door against disturbances at an angle of 30 degrees for a very long time, his muscles would continually fatigue, reducing their sensitivity to neural signals and thus continually reducing the error sensitivity of this control system. But the door would remain very nearly at its reference condition until just before the end; only when the muscles have lost *most* of their sensitivity to neural stimulation will the door finally begin to yield appreciably to disturbances. After that point is reached, only a slightly greater disturbance or a few more minutes of loss of error sensitivity will result in an apparently sudden collapse of the ability to hold the door at its reference position. In truth, the decline in error sensitivity has been continual, but the properties of the control system have concealed that decline.

Given a control system with high error sensitivity, what would happen if the door were initially nearly shut, but the reference signal in the driver's brain were equivalent to an angle of 80 degrees? The error would be 80 degrees. At an error sensitivity of 10,000 grams per degree, the driver would exert an initial force on the door of 800 kilograms, or about 1,760 pounds! In other words, the driver would be pushing as hard as possible, whatever that limit is. The door would fly violently open and probably ruin the hinges and the front fender.

There are many ad hoc solutions to this problem, involving variable control of speed and nonlinearities with just the right properties, but they are all complex in comparison to the one I propose. I assume that in most human control behaviors, error sensitivity is very high, so high that under

0349558

normal conditions there is essentially 0 error at all times. To take care of the deleterious effects of too much error, I simply assume that reference signals normally vary continuously, not in an on-off manner.

If reference signals normally change continuously instead of in jumps, and if ordinary rates of change are limited enough, the control system receiving a changing reference signal can keep its sensory analogue of the controlled variable matching the reference signal at all times. When the driver grasps the door and "opens" it, I assume that he starts with a reference signal corresponding to nearly closed, and smoothly increases that reference signal to the magnitude which corresponds to fully opened. The highly sensitive control system which is involved in this action keeps the sensory analogue of the door angle matching this smoothly increasing reference signal at all times, so the door opens in a manner that exactly reflects the smoothly increasing reference signal. Once the reference signal has reached the magnitude representing the intended final angle, it ceases to change, and the control system then maintains the angle essentially at the specified reference angle, countering all disturbances. The behavior we see does not represent a process of error correction, but changes in reference signals. The only time we would see the process of error correction itself would be right after a very large and sudden disturbance.

An Important Illusion

If no disturbances were acting, the driver could hold the door at a reference-position of 45 degrees without using any effort, either push or pull. The sensory analog of the controlled variable would then exactly match the reference signal. Let us consider now the relationship between a pushing or pulling effort and a gradually increasing disturbance, assuming high error sensitivity in this control system and a constant reference signal.

As the disturbance begins to increase from 0, the error begins to increase, too, just enough to balance the push or pull against the disturbance. The system is always in equilibrium, because any less effort would allow the error to increase, creating more effort, and any more effort would decrease the error and the effort. If the error sensitivity is high enough, the error will never become significant in proportion to the reference setting, and the controlled variable will not change appreciably.

For all practical purposes, therefore, the door will remain at an angle of 45 degrees, and as disturbances come and go, efforts will appear in the driver's arm muscles to create pushes and pulls that are always equal and opposite to the disturbance. If there is a steady disturbance, the muscles will produce a steady force. If the disturbance is sudden and brief, the muscles will produce a sudden and brief opposing effort. The appearance will be exactly as if the disturbance acted as a stimulus to the man's nervous system, causing a pushing or pulling movement. This appearance, this illusion, is the basis for the model that has been used in all the life sciences since their beginnings. Even Descartes used it 340 years ago.

Organisms do not *react*. They *act*, and their actions always control some set of sensed variables inside or outside the organism. Every behavior that seems to be a simple reaction to a stimulus can be seen, on more careful examination, to control some variable; the apparent stimulus can be seen to involve a disturbance of that same variable. While there may be exceptions to this principle, I believe they are few and relatively unimportant.

A Hierarchy of Control

We now have the ingredients with which to build a more complex model, one capable of representing behavior organized out of many detailed behaviors at many levels. The examples in Table 1 can help to show how a hierarchical model would be built.

Consider the adjustment of the rear view mirror. The point of changing the angle of the mirror is not to achieve any particular angle, but to center the image of the car's rear window. To center this image, a number of actions must take place. First, the driver must reach up and grasp the mirror.

Then he must exert a twisting force to overcome the friction of the mirror mount without causing a sudden large movement. The force must then be varied in whatever way is required to make the image move toward the selected position.

Raising the hand to the mirror involves smoothly changing at least three reference signals, those defining the position of the hand in a three-dimensional space. These reference signals are altered from some beginning settings to some final settings. The efforts generated by the muscles keep the perceived coordinates of the hand (in some informal subjective coordinate system) matching those defined by the reference signals; three control systems, each controlling one dimension of this sensed position, would suffice.

We can now ask what is causing these reference signals to vary. The answer can be seen in common sense: they are varying to get the hand into the right relationship with the mirror to grasp it. The signals that are reference signals with respect to one set of control systems must indicate the *actions* of a higher-level system. This higher-level system senses the relationship of hand to mirror as it exists at each moment, compares this relationship to a reference-relationship, and converts the error into a shift in lower-level reference signals. That is all it can do—it cannot run any muscles directly.

The lower-level systems simply strive to keep their respective controlled variables matching the reference signal each is receiving from the higher-level system. If the higher-level system emits a fixed set of reference signals, the lower-level systems maintain the hand in a fixed position. If the higher-level system emits a changing reference signal, the lower-level systems, still keeping the sensed position matching this reference, produce a correspondingly changing hand position.

The lower-level systems, in other words, do not have to know anything about movements or relationships. They need only sense and control position, maintaining the position error as small as possible at all times. Any reasonable disturbance, such as the weight and inertia of the arm being moved, will be counteracted by the position control systems; the higher-level system that senses and controls a relationship never senses the effect of such disturbances, since those effects are cancelled at the lower level.

The higher-level system is sensing the same situation that the position-control systems are sensing; in fact, it must be receiving copies of the sensory signals indicating position, the same sensory signals being controlled by the lower-level systems. These signals contain information about hand position, which is one of the elements from which the sense of a relationship between the hand and something else is constructed. While it would be foolish to propose too detailed a model at this early stage of developments, it seems reasonable to think that higher-level systems in general perceive an environment that is made up of lower-level sensory signals, some of which are under control by lower-level systems and thus can be manipulated by adjusting reference signals that reach those lower-level systems. A higher-level sensory signal is derived from a set of lower-level sensory signals through continuous computing processes, so that the higher-level sensory signal presents a continuous report on the status of some aspect of the lower-order world, an aspect no lower-level system can sense.

I use the term *perception* to refer to signals derived from lower-level sensory signals. In this model, perception begins with the signals generated by sensory nerve-endings. Then there are successive stages of perception, each resulting from some continuous computing process that creates new signals depending on lower-level signals in regular, if complex, ways. The external world is not only represented in the brain; it is re-represented many times, each new level of representation being derived from those of lower level.

Along with each level of representation goes a level of control. At any given level there may be many control systems—hundreds or even thousands, although not all would be active in every situation. Each control system receives a reference signal from the next higher level, and makes its own perceptual signal match that reference signal by altering reference signals for many lower-level systems. The picture is actually more complex than that, because many control systems may act at the same time by adjusting reference signals for a common set of lower-level systems; each lower-level system then receives only a *net* reference signal, and obviously does not maintain its perception at the setting demanded by *any* higher order system. It can be shown, however, that if the simultaneously active higher-level systems sense independent aspects of the set of lower-order perceptions, each can still control its own perception independently of what the others at the same level are doing, even though no system of that level can uniquely determine the reference signal for any lower-level system. For more details, consult a textbook on analogue computing, and see the methods for solving simultaneous equations.

Under the old model, which also is hierarchical in organization, a higher-level system sends command signals to lower-level systems. These command signals are elaborated by the lower-level output processes into ever-more-detailed commands, until finally the lowest level is reached, and the commands are turned into muscle tensions. Those muscle tensions cause the movements which we call behaviors.

Under the control-system model, the command signals sent by a higher-level system to a lower one do not command any actions. They *specify perceptions.* The action taken by a lower-level control system will depend not just on this command signal but on the present state of the lower-level perceptual signal and on the amount and direction of any disturbances that may be acting to alter that perceptual signal. There need be no correlation between the motor activities and the command signal, for the command is not to do, but to sense.

However many levels there are in an actual human hierarchy, we can say two things about them with confidence. First, there is not an infinite number of levels; in fact I have been able to identify only ten, even by allowing myself considerable leeway. Second, the reference signals reaching the highest-level systems do not come from higher-level systems; by definition, there aren't any higher-level systems. The first observation does not constitute a problem, but the second does.

My answer to the problem of source for the highest level

of reference signals is essentially to ignore it. If the system as a whole is organized as a hierarchy of control systems, the highest reference signals have to come from somewhere unless they are all identically 0. (Lack of a reference signal has the same effect as setting a reference signal to 0: the concerned control system then acts to reduce its perceptual signal to 0 and keep it there.) If the reference signals exist and come from somewhere that is not another level of control systems, they must come from some built-in source, or from previous experience via memory storage, or from somewhere else. It does not seem important right now to decide on the answer. Since a few reasonable answers are available, we can tentatively assume that magic is not involved.

To understand how the entire hierarchy of control works, one must try to imagine all levels in operation at the same time. Of necessity, the higher-level systems work on a slower time-scale than the lower ones; the greater complexity of perceptual processes introduces delays, and the requirement of maintaining stability (freedom from spontaneous self-sustained oscillations that destroy control) despite these delays demands even further slowing and smoothing of higher-level activities. As far as any higher-level system is concerned, the response-time of a lower-level system is 0; the perception being specified by the reference signal sent to the lower-order system varies *as* the reference signal setting is altered. Any lag in lower-level actions is necessarily shorter than the lag in a higher-level system. The higher-level system necessarily contains smoothing filters that average out any changes that occur over intervals comparable to its lag-time, so that lag-time appears to the system itself to be 0. Thus each level involves a "specious present," a definition of "an instant," which is longer than for a lower-level system. From the perspective of the system that establishes the relationship "hand grasping mirror," the transition from the initial relationship to that final one requires no time.

The lowest level of behavioral control systems (as opposed to biochemical control systems, which are not treated here) is the spinal reflex. A spinal reflex is actually a closed loop of cause and effect in which a muscle has effects on a sensory nerve via a short path through the environment, so short that most reflex loops can be traced entirely within the skin of an organism. The bulk of these first-level control systems involves the control of sensed muscle effort. The comparator for a spinal control system is a motor neurone in the spinal cord; this neurone receives a sensory signal from something affected by the muscle, and also a large set of convergent "command" signals from higher in the nervous system. The effect of an increased command signal is uniformly either an increase in the inhibiting effect of a feedback signal, or a decrease in the exciting effect of a feedback signal. In both cases, negative feedback results and the organizational requirements for control are satisfied. The signal leaving the spinal cord and going to a muscle, the so-called "final common pathway," is actually the error signal of the control system. There is one such control system for every voluntary muscle in the body.

While an upper boundary for this hierarchy is hard to define, the lower boundary is clear. As far as overt behavior is concerned, there are no systems lower than the spinal reflexes, the level-one systems. Level 0 is the outside world. All action is carried out by specifying settings for the reference signals entering level-one control systems. These reference signals do not tell those systems what to do; they tell them how much tension to *sense.*

A Possible Human Hierarchy

In the following pages, I will present 10 levels of perception (and by implication, control) that I think are reasonable guesses about our actual construction. Each level is defined as a *class* of perception. What I assume is that the brain, at birth or before, contains these levels in the form of specialized types of computing networks. Within one level there are initially no perceptual signals corresponding to the elements of adult experience; instead there are the materials from which can be constructed neural functions of particular types. Some levels, for example, may require short-term memory; if that proves to be so, the neural components required to construct short-term memory devices are present, although not yet connected in any useful way.

I assume that in an adult person, there are specific devices at each level, each device being physically connected so as to receive certain lower-level perceptual signals and to compute on a continuous basis the value of some function of those signals; the computed value is the next level of perceptual signal. We are not born with these specific devices; they are constructed on the basis of experience with lower-level signals created by contact with the environment into which the person is born. The construction does not, of course, involve the creation of any new neurones; it is done by creating new connections among the fixed set of neurones we inherit.

Classes of perceptions are created simply because the brain is layered into classes of potential computing devices. A level-two perceptual function, I assume, cannot ever perform a level-three perceptual function simply because level two of the brain does not contain the required types of neurones or interconnecting pathways. We inherit, therefore, the potential of perceiving certain fixed classes of experience, although we do not inherit the ability to perceive any particular items at a given level. If this assumption is correct, we should find that all normal adults, in any culture, of any race, in any occupation, or with any degree of education, will experience a world made up of these same categories (although of course with highly varied examples within each category). A mathematician from Harvard and an African pigmy will have the same levels from lowest to highest; they will differ only in the way those levels have become organized: in content, not form.

There is, of course, another possibility. Perhaps if levels of perception exist, it is because reality is organized the same way and we have merely evolved to perceive what is really there. I would have to see a proof of "what is really there" before I could accept that, however.

Let us now look at these proposed levels.

1. *Intensity.* Level-one perceptions are the signals generated by sensory nerve endings. As the intensity of stimulation increases, the frequency of firing of sensory nerves increases.

Whether this relationship be direct or transient, first-level perceptual signals themselves can vary only in one dimension: frequency. Thus each such signal can carry only magnitude information, there being no way for one signal to carry, in addition, identification of the source.

These signals can be experienced subjectively. They accompany every modality of experience. They are experienced simply as *intensity,* without regard to kind. It is perfectly possible to judge, using higher-level processes, the relative intensity of a sound and a light, a process which makes no use of any information about the sound or the light except *how much* of each is present.

Intensity signals that are under control are primarily kinesthetic; we call them *effort,* meaning not directed effort but simply amount of effort. When we pick up an object, we judge its weight largely by the effort-intensity signals created by picking it up. If a large effort-intensity signal results, we say the object is heavy.

Most intensity signals are not under significant control at level-one. They pass on to level two where all intensity signals are received and, through neural computations typical of level two, are transformed into sensations.

2. *Sensations.* I define a sensation as a weighted combination of intensities. I mean by this term what is ordinarily meant: color, taste, sound, force, and all such elementary experiences. Most sensation-signals are not under direct control, but their hierarchical relationship to intensities is not hard to see. There can be no sensation of color if there is no light intensity experienced, but the reverse is not true. Thus color sensations depend on combinations of visual intensity signals from receptors in the retina, an assertion that should not startle anybody.

A common sensation is *warmth.* If a warm object (known to be warm, of course, by the way it feels) is moved over the skin, many different intensity signals come and go but there remains *one* unchanging sensation of warmth. The identification of the experience as warmth is independent of *which* warmth receptors contribute to the level-two perceptual signal. A sensation signal is appreciated as a *quality* of experi-

ence. We experience cold as different from warmth not necessarily because different receptors are involved, but perhaps
because different weights are assigned to intensity signals and
different signals result. It is hard to describe the difference
between cold and warm sensations, but one is clearly *here*
while the other is *there*, in some sort of experiential scale.

Kinesthetic   sensations   amount   to   directed   vectors.
Common level-two kinesthetic sensations are push, pull,
twist, and squeeze, sensed not in relationship to anything else
but simply as familiar sensations. These coordinated sets of
efforts are organized in the brain stem. It is interesting that
we can experience them so easily.

3. *Configuration.* While it is easy to experience the world
as being totally filled with sensations, it is next to impossible
to prevent these sensations from grouping themselves into
recognizable associations, i.e., configurations. In the visual
modality, we call some of these configurations *objects.*
Others are simply arrangements of parts of a space against the
background of other parts. The Gestalt concept of figure and
ground applies at this level.

To control a configuration, it is necessary to alter some set
of sensations. For the driver of the car to create the familiar
configuration made by the image of the rear window in the
rear view mirror, it is necessary to alter the detailed visual
sensations involved in the image of the scene on his retinas
(and, of course, to alter many kinesthetic sensations). On the
other hand, it is clearly possible to alter all those same sensations without creating that particular visual configuration—
and for that matter, without aiming at any particular configuration. If the visual sensations of edge, shading, and color
were not present, no visual configuration could exist, since
sensations are the elements of configurations. Thus from the
standpoint of which kind of perception depends on which,
and from the standpoint of which must be altered to control
which, configurations are at a higher level in the hierarchy
than sensations.

There are configurations in every sensory modality. They
are the least units of experience that can be shown to depend
on the existence of at least two different sensations, and the

control of which depends on altering sensations.

The world of configurations is static, in the sense that maintaining a configuration at a fixed reference level results in a static situation. A system controlling a configuration (or one dimension of it) may be quite active as disturbances fluctuate or as its reference signal changes, but we judge the nature of a level of perception and control by the state of the perception when the reference level is fixed, not by the nature of the output actions of the system.

4. *Transitions.* When we experience a series of configurations that are carried from one to the next by some regular transformation, the result is a perception that is not a configuration but a sense of movement or change. The driver backing out of the driveway, looking back through the partly-opened door, controls this sense of movement by combined use of the accelerator and brake, backing out at a *speed* that matches some reference-speed. A pianist executing a run controls the rate of change of pitch heard from the piano. A person who has just touched a hot frying pan is relieved to feel the pain *diminishing* by holding his finger under cold water. The stagehand at the control panel makes one spotlight fade at just the right speed and another increase in brightness, effecting a smooth transition from one color to another while holding brightness constant. A sportscaster slows the speed with which he is forming words to achieve a higher-level goal: finishing just as the second hand reaches the exact minute mark.

A controlled transition is a transition of lower-level perceptions at a particular rate; the reference signal for a transition-controlling system governs the speed of the transition without regard to beginning or end points. Obviously there can be no transitions if there are no lower-level perceptions, nor if the perceptions that exist remain the same. To control a transition, it is necessary to vary lower-level perceptions, yet lower-level perceptions can vary without any transition being controlled. Thus transitions are at a higher level than the perceptions which, by changing, give rise to the sense of transition.

I should mention a problem that is often raised in connection with fast transitions such as playing a run on a piano. It is possible for a level-four system to issue a series of configuration reference signals to the systems controlling the fingers faster than those systems can work. By *exaggerating* the reference signals, the level-four system can create large enough error signals in the third-level systems to result in the needed finger-movements, the reference signals being switched before the lower-order errors have come close to being corrected. (Actually, to correct them might entail breaking a finger or pulling a muscle loose.) Such extremely rapid transitions, therefore, are produced with very little lower-level control. The transition-controlling system can operate smoothly since the speed is not varying more rapidly than the control system's abilities can handle, but the lower-level systems are operating with very large error signals, and in fact are unable to maintain good control. We do not hear that lack of control, because of course we cannot perceive on a fast enough time scale to notice what the pianist cannot sense either.

5. *Sequence.* When the driver shifts from first gear into reverse, he grasps the gearshift, depresses the clutch, moves the gearshift forward, and releases the clutch slowly while gradually increasing the pressure on the accelerator pedal. Thus backing up the car involves control of perceptions at all levels through transitions—and at least at one more level. These individual actions will not result in backing the car unless they are performed in a particular sequence. Certain configurations must occur before others. Transitions must occur at the right speed, and they must occur in the right place in the sequence. Several lower-order control actions must occur simultaneously at certain places in the sequence.

There is thus a fifth level of perception and control, which I call the sequence level. A common name for familiar short sequences is *event*. (Note that the spoken word "event" is an event.) A level-five system perceives the lower-order world in terms of *what event is in progress*. Errors are seen as deviations from the "shape" of the event in space and time and are opposed by adjustments of reference signals for transition-controlling systems. (Those systems, in turn, produce the required changes in configuration, sensation, and intensity.) For a pianist to execute the run on a piano just mentioned, his level-five system need only perceive that this event is progressing properly, making small adjustments in the speed reference signal as required to maintain the event in its proper state (the state specified by a higher-order system).

I assume that for each event we have learned to recognize there is a separate perceptual function adapted to see the lower-level world in terms of that event. This is the general assumption; a perceptual function reports the state of the lower-level world, or that portion from which it receives copies of perceptual signals, as one single perception. Its output, the perceptual signal it generates, indicates by its magnitude the degree to which that one aspect of the lower-level world is present. Thus a given set of transitions and so on could easily result in perceptions of many different events at the same time—but generally only one of those perceptions will be large enough to matter. There may be a mutual inhibitory effect among perceptions of a given level, as occurs in the retina, so that the largest perceptual signal tends to suppress smaller ones at the same level, increasing the contrast between a strong impression of one sequence and weak impression of another, and similarly at any level.

Events are at a higher level in the hierarchy than any of the levels already discussed, for the same reasons. A uniformly spinning wheel exhibits transition without creating the sense of an event, but there can be no event unless there is some change of transition. To control an event requires altering transitions, but the reverse is not true.

6. *Relationships.* Shifting into reverse and beginning to back the car out of the driveway might be perceived as one event, in the case of an experienced driver. As this event proceeds, it must be maintained in proper relationship to many other events: looking back, opening the door, cars passing by, children riding bicycles, and so on. The term *relationship* is the one of importance at level six.

It is hard to explain what is meant by relationship without using the word relationship. It seems clear that there can be no *controllable* relationship unless the items related are potentially independent of each other. At least two items of experience must be involved. Relationships are defined by the way the behavior of one element of experience covaries with another element of experience. To say that a cup is *on* a saucer is to name a relationship we would not see if we perceived the cup and saucer as being carved from a single piece of material.

At all the lower levels of perception, one can find examples by casual examination of the world outside. Those examples—an event like the explosion of a firecracker, for instance—seem to be objective; they exist and need only be noticed. Relationships are not quite so easy to see as something having an independent existence. Of course it is easy to see that a cup is on a saucer, but it is hard to define just where that "on-ness" is. It isn't really anywhere.

This same problem actually exists at all the lower levels; we don't notice it because we don't normally ask questions like "where on the apple is its shape?" or "exactly when does a golf swing begin?" At the relationship level, it becomes more obvious that the observer is introducing something into the lower-level world of perception that would not otherwise be seen there.

If one says that a certain candy bar tastes sweeter than another, he asserts a relationship along the dimension of sweetness, the relationship called *greater than*. One perception of sweetness is more pronounced than another. This is clearly a judgment, a subjective perception. But at this level, the distinction between subjective and objective becomes uncertain. If a saccharimeter is used to determine degree of sweetness, an experimenter may well feel that an objective relationship has been found, because the meter indicated "2" for one candy bar and "3" for another. This way of achieving objectivity, however, only changes the perceptions; it does not do away with the need for someone to perceive a relationship, in this case the fact that "3" is greater than "2." There is no way to point to a meter and show where this relationship is. It is a perceptual interpretation.

We seem to be crossing a boundary at this level, but that is only a matter of custom and habit. A close enough look at any level would reveal the same problem. What we identify as familiar items of experience in an objective world dissolve into their lower-level elements on close inspection, and their existence becomes plainly a matter of how we choose or are organized to perceive.

One familiar kind of relationship is involved in what we term an *operation,* in the sense of an action that affects something else. By dialing a telephone, we can create the perception of a preselected voice—most of the time. By setting an alarm clock we can create the perception of a buzzer eight hours later. By pressing down on one end of a crowbar, we can make two pieces of lumber separate at the other end.

This kind of relationship perception enables us to control one perception as a means of controlling another. In most such cases, we do not perceive *how* this comes about; we simply know that if one perception is brought to a particular reference state, a related change will occur in another perception. We perceive cause and effect, but not the processes that bring it about. Nevertheless, we can control such relationships, since we have the ability to vary one or more of the related elements to counteract changes that we cannot control in the rest of the elements. A cat chasing a mouse cannot control the movements of the mouse, but by altering its own motions, it can control the relationship between itself and the mouse. Even cats have some level-six systems.

Relationships perceived at this level can vary from the elementary ("toward") to the complex ("mother"), from the formal ("exclusive or") to the informal ("nicer"). Most relationships that we control are probably perceived but not named; the relationship, for example, between oneself and a partially-opened door through which one is squeezing, or between a fork and a pile of scrambled eggs one is eating. To perceive and control relationships one does not have to talk about them; talking is a different sort of activity. Most of what we perceive and control at all levels is nonverbal; it's just that some of us tend to limit our conscious attention to the verbalizations.

Relationships are of higher level than events, by the same criteria we have been using. It may be a good exercise for the reader to apply them explicitly.

7. *Categories.* This level did not appear in my 1973 book, and it may not survive much beyond this appearance. The only reason for its introduction on a trial basis is to account for the transition between what seems to be direct, silent control of perceptions to a mode of control involving symbolic processes (level 8).

A category or class is truly a disembodied entity. If I perceive a familiar shape, I might call it "Fido," or I might call it "a dog." If I call it "Fido" I mean to point to a particular configuration, that one right over there, my dog. If I call it "a dog," however, I am really not pointing to that dog at all. I am indicating a *class* of perceptions of which that particular one is only an example. If I say, "A dog will eat dog food," I do not mean that *my* dog, that one there, would eat dog food if I set it down in front of him—my dog might be full at the moment. I mean that the class of items called dogs performs the class of activities called eating relative to the class of items called dog food. I am speaking in classes, not specifics.

To know what class name to apply in any given case, it is necessary first to be able to distinguish among classes, perceptually. Should I call that relationship "racing" or "fleeing"? I cannot pick the name until I have made a perceptual identification. I make the identification by examining an array of relationships, and if the relationships make a familiar pattern, I "recognize" the category, after which I can come up with its name.

It is often said that classes or categories are established by looking for something which different items have in common. I think that is backwards. What we really do is to establish first the idea of a class, say items with "one broken leg," and then look to see if the items at hand can be perceived as members of that class. By working back and forth between lower levels and the category level, we often can come up with a familiar category that can then be exemplified by all the items being examined. The general concept of "one broken leg" has to be organized as a mode of perception before we can see if anything, even a single item, belongs to that category.

Many useful categories are formed so that their lower-level examples entail clearly recognizable perceptions of the same kind. This is definitely not true of all categories, however, which is why I am rejecting the usual concept of common elements as the determinant. Consider the category of things that are "mine," or things that are "expensive," or things that are "not here." A category is basically an *arbitrary* way of grouping items of experience; we retain those that prove useful.

This means that we can quite easily treat items as members of the same category even though we see nothing in common among them. The particular example I am thinking of, and the main reason initially for considering this as a level of perception, is the category which contains a set of perceptions (dog 1, dog 2, dog 3, dog 4 . . .) and one or more perceptions of a totally different kind ("dog," a spoken or written word). Because we can form *arbitrary* categories, we can symbolize. The perception used as a symbol becomes just as good an example of a category as the other perceptions that have been recognized as examples.

A symbol is merely a perception used in a particular way, as a tag for a class. The perception of a particular class can then be evoked as easily by that tag as by any of the other perceptions that are also perceived as examples of that class. The process also works the other way; if I ask, "Have you ever had one of those?" and point to Fido, you will understand that I am asking if you have ever had "a dog."

At this level maps and territories begin to get confused. If one too regularly confines attention to perceptions of this level or higher, he may forget that treating different items in terms of the category to which they belong is ignoring the differences making them unique. Those differences become evident only if all levels of perception are equally available to awareness.

To speak of "control" of a category may seem strange if one thinks of it in the same way as control of position. Remember that to control something is basically to do what is necessary to create a specified perception of that something. When we come to the category level, the states of perceptions tend to become black-and-white; either this category is exemplified, or it is not. This is a dog, or it is not a dog. So to control a perception of category may require nothing more than to bring about one example of it in lower-order perception, perhaps just by looking in the right direction, or perhaps by going through lower-order actions that will reveal critical perceptions resulting in perceiving one category rather than another. ("I am looking for a nice dog for my nephew.")

Finally, it may seem that establishing a category-perception must involve a very complex and mysterious computing process. I don't think so; I think the process is almost trivially simple. All that is necessary is to "or" together all the lower-order perceptual signals that are considered members of the same category. The perceptual signal indicating presence of the category is then created if any input is present. In fact this process is so simple that I have doubts about treating it as a separate level of perception, despite its importance. The logical "or," after all, is just another relationship. It may be that categories represent no more than one of the things a relationship level can perceive.

8. *Programs.* The reason I want category perceptions to be present, whether generated by a special level or not, is that the eighth level seems to operate in terms of symbols and not so interestingly in terms of direct lower-level perceptions. At this level, we have what are called *contingencies.* If one relationship is contingent on another—if a grapefruit will fit in to a jar only if its diameter is smaller than that of the jar's mouth—we can establish the contingent relationship if the other it depends on is also present.

To perceive in terms of contingencies, one must understand a branching network of possibilities. *If* condition A holds, take branch 1; otherwise take branch 2. Some kind of *test* is implied as part of the perceptual process.

I don't want to try too hard to make this level fit the pattern of the others. Perhaps it is best merely to say that this level works the way a computer program works and not worry too much about how perception, comparison, reference signals, and error signals get into the act. I think that there are control systems at this level, but that they are constructed as a computer program is constructed, not as a servomechanism is wired.

For example, perceptual processes can be constructed to rely quite specifically on rational computing processes. I see a green Ford in the street. It has Missouri license plates. There is a steaming puddle between its front wheels, and its grill is mangled. Aha, I think, somebody from out of town has had an accident. That statement amounts to a perception of the situation constructed out of lower-level perceptions by a process that must be called reasoning. That perception appears as a string of symbols. I may then realize that it is my civic duty to report the accident (civic duty representing a reference signal from a higher level) and decide to call the police. That decision, of course, specifies not a particular action but a *class* of actions: my eighth-level system has selected a reference signal for my seventh-level systems. It is then up to my seventh-level systems to find specific relationships and events that will provide a perception of the class, "calling the police." If there is a policeman passing by I can call out to him; otherwise I might use the telephone.

Here is another example. An engineer has the responsibility for maintaining the density of a batch of paint at a constant level. He records the volume of paint in a container and the weight of the paint plus container. Subtracting the weight of the container, he gets the weight of the paint, and by dividing the weight by 32 times the volume he obtains the density as a number. All of this is done through manipulation of symbols, on paper or in his head. He then compares that number with a reference-number, subtracts to obtain the difference, and, depending on whether the difference is positive or negative, adds solvent or pigment to the container. He repeats this process until the density is what it should be.

This is a perfectly good control system; it simply works in terms of computations carried out in symbols instead of lower-level perceptions. People can obviously do this sort of thing; therefore they obviously need a level of organization capable of performing the necessary operations. I can't think of a better reason for putting this level into the model. Miller,

Galanter, and Pribram (1960) proposed a whole model of human organization based on this sort of programmed control concept.

Operations of this sort using symbols have long been known to depend on a few basic processes: logical operations and tests. Digital computers imitate the human ability to carry out such processes, just as servomechanisms imitate lower-level human control actions. As in the case of the servomechanism, building workable digital computers has informed us of the operations needed to carry out the processes human beings perform naturally—perhaps not the *only* way such processes could be carried out, but certainly *one* way, which is better than not knowing any. Knowing one arrangement of components that can imitate aspects of human reasoning, we can be confident that reasoning is not carried out by little men in our heads or by magic; we can accept it as part of our understanding of human nature without defying physics or any other set of principles we have reason to accept.

There is one problem which experience with digital computers has revealed very clearly. Any machine that can be programmed can be programmed in an extremely large number of different ways; for a human brain, or even just one of many levels of organization in it, that number is for all practical purposes infinite. Among the infinity of programs that might run in the human eighth level of organization are *hierarchically organized* programs. Furthermore, any system which we are capable of understanding can be *simulated* in a computer: the physical variables can be represented by variable numbers, and the relationships among the physical variables can be replaced by computations. Thus the entire hierarchy we have been looking at could be repeated as a program in our eighth-order systems. Indeed, isn't that what we have been doing here?

Worse than that: not only this hierarchy, but any other could be simulated, including a hierarchy with 200 levels, or 2,000, or 2. These hierarchies, if debugged, could run quite successfully, and the person programmed this way at the eighth level could act as if his brain were organized, wired, as the program is organized, at least as far as his symbol-manipulating activities were concerned.

I call this a problem (it is also a tremendous advantage for us) because of the confusion it generates among those who try to model the organization of human beings. Most of the models I know about are not really models of the brain like the one we have been going through; they are models of programs that can run at the eighth level of a brain. Semantic network analysis is that sort of thing. Miller, Galanter, and Pribram's TOTE unit is that sort of thing. Most abstract mathematical models, even those under investigation by some pretty good and smart friends of mine, are that sort of thing. Studies of artificial intelligence, indeed all systems that depend primarily on qualitative and verbal reasoning, are also.

Once we know that programs can run in the brain, there is little point in getting involved with the question of *what* programs can run. That is an interesting question, but here we are trying to identify levels of organization that *must* be there, not those that represent only happenstance culturally supplied information content. If there is a level of the brain that can be programmed by stored information, that level can behave like any conceivable organization: hierarchy, heterarchy, stimulus-response robot, or Turing Machine. It can be programmed to behave rationally or irrationally. It can be programmed as a positive feedback system that destroys itself as soon as it acts. None of those details tell us more than we knew when we realized that programs can run in a brain.

When we get to the subject of development, by the way, I think it will be clear that studying programs can be quite important when the point is to investigate one person's capabilities.

9. *Principles.* We now go beyond the levels where I think there is clear justification for assumptions. If there is a level higher than the program level, it would be the level that perceives something exemplified by many different programs, and specifies objectives for the program level to accomplish. Naturally, since the program level can be and probably is organized hierarchically, it is not easy to specify a higher level that is not just another level of programming, but I think

it can be done.

The sort of perceptual level we are after is the kind one would use in evaluating a program, or in choosing one program over another. This program, one might say, is inefficient; that one is clumsy; the next is elegant; the last violates privacy. Considerations come into play that have nothing to do with any particular program.

I have chosen the term *principle* to characterize perceptions of the ninth level. There must be a better word, but this one will have to do for now. The meaning I intend is in the sense of *principle of operation*, as would be perceived when one looks at a program and says, "I know that one—it calculates square roots by *successive approximation.*" Successive approximation is a principle. It is not any particular program, although particular programs which are examples of it can certainly be devised. Once one has understood the strategy of successive approximation, one can recognize it in any disguise. As far as I know, nobody has been able to write a program which, by itself, could obey the command "Use successive approximation!" Programs just can't generalize in that way. Programmers, however, can.

Another way to think of the ninth level might be this. Suppose there is a square root (or a shopping-for-potatoes) program in operation. At the program level, the activities would involve manipulating symbols according to preprogrammed rules and applying contingency tests at appropriate places. Nowhere in that program, however, is anything capable of characterizing the program that is running; the program is running, not characterizing. For a person to *describe* the program, it would be necessary for a point of view to exist from which the program could be seen in operation—and that would have to be outside the program.

However many levels of hierarchically organized programming are running, there is a highest level. In order to characterize that level, a person needs a point of view that is higher still: that is, higher than the program level itself. That higher level selects first this executive program and then that one, to bring about perceptions that may include programs themselves as elements, but which are not of their nature. This higher level would decide, for example, "I'm never going to solve this problem by thinking; it's time to try something at random."

In that unfinished state, we leave level nine.

10. *System concepts.* We now venture onto shaky ground indeed. I think that one more level is needed to take care of a perception that still seems missing. Consider not the word "I," but that entity to which the word refers, for you. The referent of this word consists of essentially all we have been through, *plus* something else, which I call a system concept. If I say the word "physics" to a physicist, he knows what it means: a system of principles, procedures, relationships, events, and so on to the bottom. But these elements all comprise a *system,* not an assortment. It hangs together, creates the impression of one organized entity. We have many words—not many in comparison to other kinds, but quite a few—which point to an experience we all recognize; the concept of a person, a country, a company, a self, a family. We can clearly tell the difference between different system concepts; each one creates a context in which everything else happens. This context is almost tangible, and sometimes is treated as if it were more tangible than its elements. (Think of a baseball team after a complete change of players, coaches, managers, owners, and city.) When the system concept in question is one's self, one will go to considerable lengths to preserve its integrity; an error signal at that level is taken very seriously. I'm not quite sure what good it does us to have and preserve reference states for system concepts, but I think we clearly do. And this is as far as my thinking has so far progressed.

Table 2 is a summary of the ten levels, with examples drawn from a number of different contexts.

A final remark, before we go on to look at applications, is in order. It may seem that all the levels higher than the first would be invisible internal processes, akin to intervening variables, and thus not directly testable. In fact all these levels can be seen in action from outside the organism. Each deals with a different aspect of the perceived world, and to the extent that all human beings perceive in about the same

TABLE 2

Some possible levels in a hierarchy of control systems

Level	General Term	Music	Physics (inanimate world)	Motor Activities	Inner Experience	Verbal Experience (auditory)	Verbal Experience (visual)
10	System	Performance	System	Occupation	Being	Communication	
9	Principle	Interpretation	Principle	Style	Attitude	Deep structure	
8	Program	Execution	Process	Technique	Thought	Grammar	
7	Category	Opus	Phenomenon	Task	Role	Semantics	
6	Relationship	Orchestration	Interaction	Operation	Interaction	Syntax	
5	Event	Phrase	Event	Pattern	Action	Word/Phrase	
4	Transition	Dynamics	Path	Motion	Change	Consonant	Direction
3	Configuration	Chord	State	Posture	Emotion	Phoneme	Letter/word
2	Sensation	Pitch	Property	Effort	Feeling	Pitch/hiss	Mark
1	Intensity	Loudness	Magnitude	Tension	Intensity	Loudness	Brightness

manner, one human being can see variables of any level being controlled just by paying attention to the right aspects of another's actions. As we shall see, all proposals about control systems in this model can be tested by acceptable experimental methods.

The ten levels we have just seen are one concept of an adult's organization, or the inherited framework within which that organization comes into being. It matters very little whether those ten levels are correct. The point of developing them has not been to construct an immense hypothesis to test in one Grand Master Experiment, but to survey the range of organizations in a human being that need to be accounted for and to get a feel for how all human activity might be handled in one consistent theory.

There are those, no doubt, who feel that efforts like these are a waste of time, but I do not agree. Psychology has, in the past, used models so elementary in their structure that it is an insult to be told they represent human beings. The hierarchical control system model represented by these ten levels is not too complex; it is still too simple. Its main advantage is that it deals with at least a respectable range of human activities without the use of a Procrustean bed, and does so in a way we have a hope of understanding.

I have laid out this hierarchy in so much detail to demonstrate an approach. Everything that I have been able to catch myself doing while constructing and using this theory is in that model. I have claimed no privileged point of view. It may well be that I have not named the levels correctly, or that under different circumstances different levels would be observed, but the existence of hierarchical control levels in which one system acts by determining the reference signals for others seems to me a sound basic hypothesis. The need to account for organized activities from spinal reflexes to rational thought and beyond seems far clearer to me now than before I had constructed these levels; I hope that is true for the reader, too.

As I said in the beginning, thinking of human organization in terms of these levels must have a strong influence on what we consider human development to be. Having seen one coherent set of levels that encompasses most aspects of human activities, perhaps it will be possible for others now to begin asking questions that will reveal better definitions or aspects of organization I have missed. There can be no better subject than the study of human development for this purpose. Let us now see how this kind of study could proceed in the light of a hierarchical control concept.

The Discovery of Control Organizations

There is, fortunately, a systematic way to test any hypothesis about human control behavior. Indeed, if that were not true, this whole theory *would* be an untestable fantasy. In a way, I have applied the method to be described here all during the development of this model, although not with the formality that must eventually be demanded. The essence of the method is a procedure to test the hypothesis that some variable is under control. With this method, one can feel much freer than otherwise to propose possible control organizations, since it will ruthlessly weed out wrong guesses.

I call this method a test for the controlled variable. It functions as follows.

Suppose that for any reason (or for no reason) one decides to test the hypothesis that variable A is controlled by a control system. Available are other physical variables B, C, D, and so on, each influencing the state of A. The nature of these influences can be found by inspection of or experiment with the variables, in the absence of any potential control system to interfere with the inspection.

The test involves nothing more than applying disturbances to the selected variable by altering other physical variables known to effect it, and verifying that the definition of control is satisfied. If it is satisfied, every influence that should affect the state of the controlled variable is met by some equal and opposite reaction from a control system; the result is that the proposed variable is stabilized against disturbances. It is not necessary, initially, to know where the control system is or what its mode of action is. The first step is always to try disturbing a proposed variable, and to see whether the resulting changes in the variable can be accounted for strictly in terms of observable physical phenomena, including the disturbance. If they can, there is no control system.

If a variable is affected far less by a disturbance than expected, something else is acting to oppose the effects of the disturbance. To be sure that this something else is a control system, one must identify the *means* of control, and also show that the variable has to be *sensed* by the system applying the means, for control to be maintained.

A Thought Experiment

Let's try this method in a thought experiment that should be familiar enough to most readers to make the conclusions seem realistic. We will occupy the passenger seat while our driver drives the car down a straight level unencumbered freeway on a windless day. One obvious hypothesis is that the driver is controlling the position of the car relative to the road.

From previous experience with cars, we know that even a small steady deflection of the steering wheel will cause a car travelling 55 miles per hour to move quickly out of its lane. Thus it would be easy to insert a disturbance; we quietly take hold of the steering wheel and exert a small force to turn it. The result is *not* the expected veering of the car, so we know that the position of the car in its lane may be related to a controlled variable.

The disturbance is clearly being counteracted by a force from the driver's arm muscles; it is not hard to discover the means being used. We shall now see why it is necessary also to check the perception that is involved.

Suppose we temporarily alter our hypothesis, because we can now see that *steering wheel position* is also being held constant and is much more directly involved in our disturbance and the driver's reaction to it. It would be hard to interrupt the driver's ability to sense steering wheel position since he can *feel* it as well as see it as long as he is holding the wheel. So let us provide a different means of control that does not involve the driver's holding onto the wheel: *we* will move the wheel according to verbal directions from the driver. Each time he says "left" we turn the wheel a little further to the left; each time he says "right," a little further to the right.

The driver won't be able to steer quite as precisely under these conditions, but we will find that he can still keep the car well within its lane with a little practice. Now, if we persuade the driver to allow a cardboard shield to be placed where it blocks his view of the steering wheel, we can cut off his means of sensing the wheel position without preventing him from *affecting* the wheel position.

With the shield in place, we test the driver's ability to resist disturbances of the steering wheel again. If we do not get too violent or make very rapid changes in the disturbance, we will find that the driver countermands every disturbance we apply independently of him. The result is that the steering wheel is never permitted to stray very much from its original position.

The test has thus been failed. Steering-wheel position is *not* a controlled variable, because the driver continues to act much as he did before even without being able to sense steering wheel position.

We could quickly establish the real nature of the controlled variable by returning to the original conditions, and this time blocking the driver's view of the road. As soon as we prevent the driver from seeing the relationship of the car to the road, control is lost. The driver may try to resist our disturbances of the wheel—he probably will—but he will not be able to cancel disturbances exactly enough to keep the car on the road. He will have switched, in fact, to controlling the sensed position of the wheel, as we could verify by adding the cardboard shield again and going to the verbal mode. In that case, control of wheel position would be lost, too, as anyone would predict who is clearly visualizing the situation.

If we were doing this in a driver-training simulator, we could narrow the definition of the controlled variable even further. In a good simulator, a computer translates the speed of the car and the steering wheel angle into appropriate changes in the visual display. By tampering with the computer, we could disturb the visual display relative to the computed position of the car, displacing the display by some small amount to the right or left of where it should be. Now we find that the computed position of the car varies every time we displace the display; what stays constant is the display, not the position of the car. The picture that the driver sees in the windshield is, or contains, the controlled variable. By fuzzing out various aspects of the display, we could eventually discover just what aspects of that picture are being sensed, and hence just what variable is under control.

Something similar could be done with speed. By surreptitiously pressing down on the accelerator, we could test the idea that the driver is controlling (a) accelerator pressure, (b) rate of change of the scene in the windshield, or (c) the speedometer reading. The reader can, of course, now design the necessary experimental details.

Exploring the Hierarchy

The above test provides a way for identifying controlled variables for a system in which the reference signal remains constant for the duration of the experiment. Once the principle is understood, this test can be carried out quite rapidly, so the reference signal need not remain constant long, but the demand for a constant reference signal does limit the application of the test in a hierarchy of systems. The reason is that in order to maintain a higher-level variable constant, a control system acts by *continually altering* lower-level reference settings. We need some way of identifying control systems of lower level than the principal one under investigation.

It is sometimes possible to identify a few lower-level organizations in natural situations, because lower-level systems always operate on a faster timescale than higher-level systems. In the case of the driver steering a straight course, we might well suspect that there is a lower-level system for controlling the position of the steering wheel, as part of the means for controlling the car-to-road relationship. Applying brief disturbances to the steering wheel, we could verify that resistive forces develop *before* any appreciable change in car position can occur. There is an initial immediate resistance, which then becomes larger, after a delay, when the car actually moves visibly in its lane. In effect, we are seeing the lower-level system operating with a constant reference signal for a short time, before the higher-level system senses an error in its variable and alters the lower-level reference signal.

This "nesting" of reaction times provides one way, probably best suited to the laboratory, for sorting control actions by level. It is not, of course, absolute; I have found, for example, that separation of levels is not good unless the control behavior is very well practiced. Clear evidence of control does not appear until learning is essentially complete.

A more general method can often give much more direct evidence of levels of control. Each level in the hierarchy deals with a different class of variable. Furthermore, at every level there are many perceptions that are *not* under control; think of the previous example of a cat controlling its relationship to a mouse without being able to control the sensed position of the mouse.

It is therefore often possible to apply disturbances which affect a system of one level without affecting systems of lower level. In the case of the driver, we have been applying disturbances that affect a possible wheel-position control system as well as the car-position system that is supposedly using that wheel-control system; it is awkward and in many cases impossible to separate the two levels using this sort of disturbance. But there are other kinds. Suppose, for example, that we had a way of keeping track of the crosswind component of any wind that was blowing, and had tables for converting that component into an effective disturbance of car position. The wind is not going to disturb the steering wheel directly; hence even if there is a wheel-control system acting, it will not be disturbed. A sudden gust will not result in an instantly appearing muscle force; only as the car begins to drift sideways will the driver's arms begin to turn the wheel to oppose the effect of the wind.

The converse can sometimes be done. If we can apply *two* disturbances, one to the steering wheel and another (applied to the car directly) continuously adjusted to keep the car's position from changing, we can prevent the higher-level system from seeing any error, and thus prevent it from altering the lower-level reference signal. In effect, we take over the higher-level control action, and are able to see the lower-level system acting with a constant reference signal. We cancel higher-level disturbances before the system we are investigating can sense their effects. We can then disturb the variable for the lower-level system without causing the higher-level error that would usually also result.

How and Why

In most ordinary behavior, a person is engaged in control activity at some particular level that is more highly visible than any other level. This most visible level is the lowest level at which the reference condition for a controlled variable is being held, for the time, constant. A person standing at a bathtub with one hand under the water faucet while the water runs is waiting, perhaps, to feel a sufficient level of warmth before stoppering the tub to fill it. For the moment, we are seeing a simple sensation-control system in operation; the hand on the cold-water handle turns the handle until a steady level of warmth is felt. What is going at a higher level is a sequence called "filling the tub," or "taking a bath." For the time being, however, all reference signals above a certain level are fixed, until the current element of the sequence appears in perception.

If we pick an example of behavior at random, we have no immediate way of saying what level of organization is visible. By asking *how* and *why*, however, we can begin to get an idea of what level we are looking at, at least in relative terms.

To ask *how* a given perception is being controlled is to ask about the *means* of control. The means, for a system above the lowest level, is always manipulation of reference signals for lower-level systems, so asking *how* is the same as asking what lower-level variables are being controlled to control the higher-level variable. *How* does the person control the sensation of warmth? By exerting muscle efforts, the hand already being properly positioned on the handle. Once higher-order systems have taken care of that positioning and have established a firm grasp, a simple two-level control system can control the warmth.

If we had started with the level of "taking a bath," asking *how* this event could be created would lead us, sooner or later, to the act of controlling warmth. Asking *how* takes us downward in the hierarchy.

Asking *why*, on the other hand, takes us upward. The meaning of "why" is not quite as unambiguous as the meaning of "how," but we will take it to mean, "for what purpose?" For what purpose is the person adjusting the warmth of the water? To fill the tub—and at least as one consideration among many, to control the transition of temperature that is felt as one first steps in. Ultimately, the purpose is to take a bath. More ultimately, to get clean. Still more ultimately (this being a hierarchy of many levels), to take care of one element of a relationship with other people.

When we ask *why* a given reference condition is being established, we automatically view that reference condition as an adjustable part of controlling some higher-level perception. In the spirit of the kind of modelling we have been doing here, one would always try to answer this *why* question in terms of the *least* upward step possible; one would not answer the question as to why a person is controlling the warmth of bathwater by saying "in order to be a civilized person," although for a given person that might be a system concept that is in fact under control by means (among other means) of taking a bath. The question *why*, as well as *how*, must be considered as unique to every individual. People take baths for all kinds of reasons. If we can map an individual's control organization, why try to characterize that person in fuzzy universal terms?

By exploring organization through asking *how* and *why*, we find details that do not commit us to any scheme of levels; we take the organizations we find. The test for the controlled variable then permits us to test hypotheses suggested by this less formal means of exploration. A fairly well defined methodology seems possible within the framework of this control model, a methodology that is quite independent of the particular levels I have proposed and which can be applied to any kind of behavior in any circumstances where the necessary observations can be made.

Let us close this chapter by looking at one way a program of research in human development might be constructed, using the tenets of this theory. In this closing section, we will finally discuss the one main field ignored until now. We now have a model of *performance* for a mature organism and ways of exploring organization. The question is now, how does that organization come about? We have to consider *learning*. I shall, however, consider it only obliquely.

Research in Human Development

I think it is clear that no person is born with a control system that controls the perception of being civilized, much less one which entails taking baths to accomplish that goal. There is no need to assume that we are born with any behavioral control systems at all, save perhaps a few constructed in the last four or five months in the womb and being centered around control of efforts.

In my 1973 book I proposed a model for learning in which a process called *reorganization* was driven by errors that signified some deviation within the organism itself: *intrinsic* error signals. The controlled variables for this reorganizing system were measures of the state of the organism; the reference conditions were inherited. The action of this system involved *altering connections* in the brain. This connection-altering process resulted in the hierarchy of control systems in an adult, and in the gradual creation of these control systems during development. The only preorganization I assumed was in the kinds of components available at various levels of the brain from which to construct the parts of control systems. The reorganizing system was not "intelligent." It did not learn from experience, nor did it seek any particular organization of the brain. All we call intelligence resided in the hierarchy of perception and control that results from reorganization.

This reorganizing system, clearly, has to be defined as what it does, not what it is. My proposals were an attempt to guess what it does. When we are talking about research in human development, however, we do not need to guess about that. We can find out by applying the principles of control theory to characterize human organization at various stages in its development and, on the basis of changes we see in that organization, we can specify what any reorganizing system must do.

My suggestions for a cybernetic research program in human development, therefore, will have nothing to say about learning theory itself. Just as most astronomers ceased to speculate about the surface of the moon once it was evident that men would soon be walking on it, I feel little urge to speculate about the process of reorganization, knowing that we will soon know more about it than we do now.

I see a program of research in human development as a series of stages we go through to build a new understanding of human nature in a systematic way. We first gather basic data in a more or less naturalistic way, data which traditional methods have not provided and could not provide. Then we try to classify this data into a taxonomy of levels—or else conclude that levels are not significant features of organization. Next, we can begin to look for patterns relating to the development of organization from very little to maximum. And ultimately, I hope we can devise efficient and accurate ways for mapping the organization of an individual from his most elementary reflexes to his overall properties. Out of that will come immense benefits. For the first time, we will be able to say just what is wrong with a person who is having troubles. We will be able to devise psychotherapeutic methods that go directly to the difficulty instead of taking years to find the trouble by a random search, or solving the problem by destroying capacities of the brain. We should be able to improve the methods of education by orders of magnitude. We should be able to match a whole person to a whole job, on the basis of specific knowledge rather than statistical comparisons with masses of other people. I have, in short, some definite and hopeful expectations about what we could do with control theory. The following are some ideas about how to get from here to there.

Gathering Data

The principal kind of data that is needed about any human being at any stage of development concerns *what variables that person can control.* If no human being controls any variables—if all hypotheses fail the test for the controlled variable—we can save ourselves a lot of trouble by abandoning the project there.

The initial effort, it seems to me, must be to accumulate experience with control behavior. I envision not just a vast effort at reinterpretation, but a systematic testing application for the controlled variable. The only data about human control behavior that will be of any use will be catalogues of controlled variables which have passed every application of the test for the controlled variable, conducted with as much rigor as possible. It does not matter if this data gathering is systematic; it may well be best to take examples at random, without regard to any proposed hierarchy or any other preconceived notions. Experimental verification of proposed controlled variables should be done with human beings of all ages, occupations, races, cultures, and so on. The greater the range of hypotheses tested, the better.

Classifying the Data

Once a sufficient amount of information is available in terms of variables proven to be controllable by human beings, the next step is to sort this information into meaningful categories. One obvious dimension of sorting is by age; at what age range does each variable become controllable? Another is by type, if that proves possible. I would be interested, of course, in types which can be shown to stand in hierarchical relationship, although any data is good data even if it does not support my organizational prejudices.

This phase will call for new kinds of data gathering, aimed at sharpening methods for distinguishing levels of organization, or for otherwise mapping relationships among control activities. There will be plenty of room for ingenuity.

Characterizing Development

There are reasons to think that in acquiring any new control organization, a person is likely to develop the parts of that system in a particular order: (1) perception: the variable to be controlled must exist as a neural analogue; (2) recording: the possible states of that variable must be experienced and remembered; (3) selection: one previous state of the variable must be selected as a reference signal; (4) comparison: the error between the actual and intended states of the variable must be judged; (5) action: the error must be converted into those changes of existing lower-level reference signals that will correct the error; and (6) practice: this entire series must be iterated over and over to refine each element of the control system so that it functions under all conditions without instability.

That is, of course, a proposal about how development of a new control system might occur. The objective of an experimental program would be to see if this sequence or any other is sufficiently universal to apply in general. If there is a preferred sequence for constructing a new control system, the implications for education or for learning skills are obvious.

More generally, the data existing by the time this phase of research became important would contain information about transitions from one organization to another. That data would contain the character of the reorganizing processes that underlie development. In traditional psychology, experiments are almost entirely concerned with learning, yet ways to characterize what is learned are as primitive as guesswork. By concentrating first on characterizing performance and organization, rather than changes in arbitrarily chosen measures, we should arrive at a learning theory that has more than statistical validity.

My hunch is that through a research program like this we will find that levels of control do exist, and that the development of a human being from fetus to adult centers around the acquisition of higher and higher levels of control and wider and wider varieties of control systems at each level. I have tried to envision a program which would not inevitably lead to that result, but which, should it uphold this hunch, would be believable on its own merits. I hope that there are others who see a challenge in this theory and this proposal and who will commence the work at hand.

References

Buckley, W. 1968. *Modern Systems Research for the Behavioral Scientist.* Chapter 5: Cybernetics, purpose, self-regulation, and self-direction. Debate with Rosenblueth, Wiener, and Bigelow on one side, and Taylor on the other in a series of papers. Chicago: Aldine. Pp. 219-242.

Maxwell, J. C. 1965. On Governors. In *The Collected Papers of James Clerk Maxwell,* W. D. Niven, ed. New York: Dover. Vol. 2, pp. 105-120.

Mayr, O. 1970. *The Origins of Feedback Control.* Cambridge, Mass.: M.I.T. Press.

Miller, G. A., Galanter, E., and Pribram, K. 1960. *Plans and the Structure of Behavior.* New York: Holt, Rinehart, and Winston.

Powers, W. T. 1973. *Behavior: The Control of Perception.* Chicago: Aldine.

Watson, J. 1919. *Psychology from the Standpoint of a Behaviorist.* Philadelphia and London: J. B. Lippincott Co. P. 13.

Wiener, N. 1948. *Cybernetics: Control and Communication in the Animal and the Machine.* New York: Wiley.

Recommended Readings

Hayek. F. 1952. *The Sensory Order.* Chicago: University of Chicago Press. 1963 Phoenix paperback. A theory of hierarchical perceptual organization predating mine, and containing many ideas I have used (without knowing they were Hayek's).

Jones, R. W. 1973. *Principles of Biological Regulation.* New York: Academic Press. A very thorough introduction to biological control systems of all kinds, with many examples and full treatment of reference signals, perceptual functions, and output processes (not in my terminology, but just as good).

McFarland, D. J. 1971. *Feedback Mechanisms in Animal Behavior.* London and New York: Academic Press. An often-cited book containing a wealth of basic examples, but little in the way of useful models. Nevertheless, a basic source.

Stevens, C. F. 1966. *Neurophysiology: A Primer.* New York: Wiley. A close look at neural functioning which is still essentially up to date. A strong antidote for the belief that neural processes are digital in nature.

3

Cybernetics, Experience, and the Concept of Self

Ernst von Glasersfeld

*Intelligence organizes the world
by organizing itself.*
—Jean Piaget

Encountering the term "cybernetics," most people tend to
think of robots, computers, and electronics. This is not surprising, considering the noise that has been made about such
gadgets and the hopes and fears associated with them. But
there is another aspect to cybernetics that, in the long run,
may turn out to be more important. When Norbert Wiener
launched the term some thirty years ago, he defined it as
"the study of control and communication in the animal and
the machine" (Wiener, 1948). Since then, this study has led
to a way of thinking about perception, behavior, and cognition that is revolutionary, not so much because of the problems it attacks, but rather because of the way in which it
views them.

I shall not say very much here about cybernetics as a discipline, but I shall adopt a cybernetic attitude and develop
some ideas on how a child forms certain basic concepts,
among them the concept of self. Drawing on Piaget's analysis
of cognitive development during the sensory-motor period, I
shall try to show, on the one hand, that his theory is quite
compatible with the cybernetic way of thinking and, on the
other hand, that the cybernetic way of thinking may help to
illuminate some of the darker corners of the theory.

There are three areas of cybernetic thought that are particularly germane to the study of early cognitive development: self-regulation, inductive learning, and the constructivist

approach to experience and its organization. The following section explicates the notions and conceptions on which much of the subsequent discussion is based.

The second section, "Piaget from a Cybernetic Viewpoint," focuses on some of the most elementary conceptual operations that, from a logical-theoretical point of view, seem to be indispensable to such concepts as *sameness, identity, continuity, space, change, motion, cause,* and *time.* The section titled "Some Basic Constructs" then outlines a tentative approach to the construct of the *experiential self* and attempts to demonstrate why the locus of active experience, the entity that embodies the experiencer, must necessarily remain outside our picture.

Much of what is said in the second and third sections can make sense only if the reader keeps in mind the points raised in the last two paragraphs of the following section. The traditional view, both in psychology and epistemology, disregards the inevitable dichotomy between what can be said about observed organisms and what an organism might be able to say about his own experience. Insofar as the cyberneticist is a builder of models (physical or conceptual) that are supposed to regulate or govern themselves, he must remain aware of that dichotomy.

CYBERNETICS AND LEARNING

Feedback and Self-Regulation

Self-regulation, in cybernetics, usually refers to the principle of "negative feedback." Some practical applications of this principle were in use more than two thousand years before its theoretical significance as an explanatory device in biology and psychology was discovered. In the simplest terms, control by means of "negative feedback" is an arrangement that enables a system (e.g., an animal or a machine) to gauge an activity according to its effect. Philon of Byzantium, in the third century B.C., built one of the earliest fully documented examples: an oil lamp in which the level of oil in the burner controlled the amount of oil fed into the burner from a reservoir (Mayr, 1970).

One of the most common examples today, a good deal more complicated in structure but embodying the same principle, is the thermostat. Here, there is a thermometer that senses the temperature in the area to be controlled. If that temperature rises beyond a preset value, a contact breaker closes and a cooling mechanism is switched on. If the temperature sinks below the set value, a heater is switched on.

To make the feedback principle quite explicit, we have to isolate its essential ingredients. There is, first of all, a sense organ that can indicate the actual temperature. Then there is the desired temperature or *reference value* that has been set by someone, and a comparator, where the sensed and the desired temperatures can be compared. As long as the reference value and actual temperature are the same, the thermostat will do nothing. But if there is a discrepancy in one direction or the other, indicating either that the actual temperature in the controlled area has been *disturbed* or that the reference value has been changed, the thermostat sends an *error signal* to activate the cooling or heating machinery, as appropriate. If everything works as expected, the temperature in the controlled area will change in the right direction, the value indicated by the sense organ will adjust to the reference value, and the error signal will cease.

The theoretical importance of these gadgets springs from the fact that they provide an irrefutable demonstration of purposive, goal-directed behavior. With that, the concept of purpose is removed from the context of Aristotelian teleology that placed it out of bounds for the modern scientist. It now has a place in the design of functioning machines and can be reinstated as a legitimate, precise, and extremely useful explanatory concept.

As a result of its technological implementations we can now also discriminate two types of purpose that, formerly, seemed inextricably confused. We can clearly see that the thermostat has the purpose *of* maintaining the temperature in the controlled area close to the reference value, whereas it is some outside agent that sets the reference value as a purpose *for* the thermostat (Pask, 1969, pp. 22-24). This distinction is of particular significance if we want to use the feedback principle to explain living organisms. While the simple arrangement illustrated by the thermostat serves well enough as a model for the homeostatic functions that control single physiological conditions in he body, such as internal temperature, sugar level, and blood pressure (see Cannon, 1932), it is obviously insufficient to explain directed behaviors whose goals change from situation to situation and from context to context.

A more sophisticated system will have a hierarchical arrangement with the reference values at one level adjusted by a control system on another level. (See, for instance, Powers, 1973). In arrangements of this sort, it will be the goal *of* one level to set the goal *for* another.

More important is the fact that the feedback model as I have so far described it does not provide for any form of learning. There are different ways of learning that can be incorporated in cybernetic models (Powers, 1973; McFarland, 1971), but one, in principle, is an implementation of the age-old process of inductive inference and was first suggested by Kenneth Craik in the early 1940s and then practically applied by Ross Ashby (1970).

Learning as a Process of Induction

The self-filling oil lamp, the thermostatic mechanism, and all similar devices that have the built-in purpose of maintaining some condition close to a pre-set reference value, are obviously the result of deliberate design. There was a designer who not only knew why he wanted a certain condition or quantity kept constant, but also how this could be achieved. The thermostat that controls the temperature in a building does not have to *learn* that it is the air conditioner that must be switched on when the sensory signal indicates a temperature above the reference value, and that it is the heating system that must be switched on in the opposite case. Since these connections are built in by the designer, the error signals that emanate from the comparator, indicating either "too hot" or "too cold," run along fixed lines to the appropriate machinery. The appropriateness of the two types of machinery, for heating and for cooling, is something that was decided by the designer on the basis of *his* prior experience and learning.

If the feedback model is to be of use in the study of the more complex forms of behavior we see in animals, and in humans, we shall have to give it some capability for learning. In Craik's words (1966, p. 59),

> We should now have to conceive a machine capable of modification of its own mechanism so as to establish that mechanism which was successful in solving the problem in hand, and the suppression of alternative mechanisms. Although this may seem a great demand, we can be comforted by the reflexion that animals and man can only modify their activity within the limits imposed by their anatomy, or the materials and machines available; though it is a great demand, it is not an infinitely great one.

In a sense, the solution lies in this very early statement of the problem. It consists in establishing and recording for every kind of error signal (problem) "that mechanism which was successful in solving the problem." In other words, if there are several kinds of *disturbance* and, consequently, several kinds of error signal, the system has to discover which of the activities in its behavioral repertoire is most likely to correct a particular error signal. On the simplest level this can be achieved only through inductive inference.

"A living system, due to its circular organization, is an inductive system and functions always in a predictive manner: what occurred once will occur again. Its organization (both genetic and otherwise) is conservative and repeats only that which works" (Maturana, 1970, pp. 15-16).

The simplest learning system, thus, will have a repertoire of several different activities and at least one sense organ and one comparator that generates an error signal whenever the sensory signals do not match the reference value. What it has to *learn* (i.e., what is not determined by fixed wiring), is to make the error signal trigger the particular activity that is likely to reduce it.

There are several other assumptions that have to be made if the system is to work. First, there must be at least one activity in the system's repertoire that can actually influence the condition represented by the sensory signals (e.g., the heating and cooling mechanisms in the thermostat). Second, the system must start out with something like a "tendency to act" whenever there is an error signal. Third, to learn, the system must be able somehow to keep track of whether or not a particular activity reduces a particular error signal; in other words, it must have some form of memory.

The first of these three assumptions is obvious and requires no explanation. The second may be questioned, but if we adopt the theory of evolution it should not be difficult to concede that organisms that, in the face of disturbance, will do *something*, have a better chance of survival than organisms that do not act at all. The third assumption is the most problematic, if only because we still have no adequate idea of what memory is and how it functions. On the other hand, we are not only certain that we humans remember past events, but that there are experiences that leave some kind of a record in other animals.

Before discussing the general implications of the learning-feedback model, there is one practical point to stress because, although it is implicit in any description of the system's functioning, its full import is rarely appreciated. The learning process necessarily begins with the random choice of an activity in response to an error signal. If that activity does not reduce the error signal, another activity will be tried, and so forth, until one is found that *does* lead to a reduction of the "disturbance." This trial-and-error procedure stops when a trial brings success. The connection between that activity and the particular error signal is then recorded and from then on, if there is no disruption, that error signal will "automatically" call up the activity that was successful. However, if there had been no disturbance and, consequently, no error signal, no learning would have taken place.

It seems quite possible, if not likely, that an organism with a fairly large repertoire of activities might have several that could reduce the same disturbance. Given the original random approach, however, the organism may not discover this. Since it has recorded that activity x was successful in eliminating a particular disturbance, it will enact this activity in response to that error signal as long as it continues to be successful, and there will be no motive to try others. One can say that such an organism will learn *only as a result of disturbance*, and it will give up or modify something it has learned only when this again leads to disturbance. This mode of functioning, as we shall see later, fits very well into the Piagetian conception of the complementary processes of *assimilation* and *accommodation*.

The Subject's Construction of Knowledge

The preceding paragraphs cover only a fraction of the work that has already been accomplished with the cybernetic approach to the analysis of regulatory functions in organisms. An excellent technical survey has been provided by McFarland (1971) and an integrated theory of behavior by Powers (1973). The epistemological aspects of the cybernetic approach have particularly interesting implications for the study of cognition and cognitive development.

The fact that we can build feedback systems capable of self-regulation within certain parameters makes it possible for us to visualize and exemplify the most elementary features of an organism's relation to its environment. For the first time we can not only ask but answer in a thoroughly operational way questions such as "What are the data of an organism's experience?" "What can and does an organism associate when it is learning?" "What constitutes knowledge in an organism, and how does it relate to the outside world?"

A learning homeostat (Ashby, 1970) may be an abominably primitive organism compared to even an amoeba. It has only one function, against several dozen in the amoeba, and it certainly cannot reproduce itself or manifest any of the other characteristics of life. Nevertheless, insofar as it is self-regulatory, it is analogous to the self-regulatory functions of the amoeba. Even if this function is carried out by completely different elements in the two systems, the logical steps involved are equivalent.

If the organism's learning is inductive, it operates on the assumption (or belief) that there must be some regularity in its experience: "what occurred once will occur again." In fact, there can be no learning without that assumption, for, as Hume put it, "If there be any Suspicion, that the Course of Nature may change, and that the past may be no Rule for the future, all Experience becomes useless, and can give rise to no inferences or Conclusions" (Hume, 1748/1963, p. 47).

Hume attributes the regularity to "the Course of Nature" and that is saying a good deal too much. The organism can afford to be more modest and assume merely some regularity in its *experience,* in the "data" or "signals" with which it operates and which, necessarily, are the only ones to which it has access. In the language of psychologists, they are the *proximal* data.

In our model the proximal data comprise the signals from the sense organ, the reference value, the error signal, and some kind of labels or signals that represent each activity in the organism's repertoire. About the last of these there are divergent views among cyberneticists, and there is certainly a need for differentiation according to the context of the activities; in one set of circumstances, for instance, one might want to speak of different *commands* that govern the activities; in another one might want to focus on *proprioceptive* signals from the parts of the oganism that are involved in carrying out the activities.

As Powers (1973) has formulated it, an organism "behaves in order to control its perception." In more explicit terms, that means that an organism acts to modify a sensory signal towards a match with the reference signal, so that there will no longer be the error signal that triggers the activity. On the simplest level we may even say that an organism acts to eliminate error signals. And its learning consists in finding (and recording for future use) an activity that will do that. The trials with different activities will cease when the error signal ceases, and the successful connection that has "caused" the reduction of the error signal will be the new "knowledge." The next time that same error signal comes from the comparator, the organism will "know" which activity to choose.

The point is that the organism has neither need nor use for what an *observer* of the organism calls its environment. Provided there is some recursion in the sequential conjunction of certain activities and certain modifications of sensory signals, the organism can learn to eliminate error signals. It needs no knowledge of distal data, of *environment*, or of an outside reality, and there seems to be no reasonable way for the organism to acquire such knowledge.

For an observer, of course, it may be plausible to establish all sorts of relations between the organism's "output," the effect of its activities on the environment, and its "input," the environmental "stimuli" that "cause" the organism's sensory signals. But these items may not be quite as straightforward as they appear. I have elsewhere argued for a radical constructivist view of knowledge (von Glasersfeld, 1975, 1976, 1977; Richards and von Glasersfeld, 1978) on all levels of organization. Here I shall confine myself to pointing out that the kind of knowledge our simple organism acquires by installing connections between error signals and activities is, indeed, a form of *construction*, and since it deals exclusively with the proximal data of the organism's own subjective experience, one would be justified in calling it wholly *subjective*. From there to Piaget's statement that "intelligence organizes the world by organizing itself" (Piaget, 1954) may not be nearly as far as it seems.

Regularities, Rules, and Explanation

If the assertion that intelligent organisms actively organize their experiential world were made by Piaget alone, one could perhaps brush it aside. Psychologists have more than once launched ideas that later turned out to be as absurd as they sounded. But while common sense and certain branches of science are still enmeshed in the realist faith of the nineteenth century, physics, the science we consider the "hardest," the least speculative, and the most dependable when it comes to empirical tests, has moved away from the belief that the knowledge we gather from experience can or even should depict an objective reality. To express the idea behind the quotation at the head of this essay, I might just as well have chosen Einstein's formulation: "It is the theory which decides what we can observe" (quoted in Heisenberg,

1971, p. 63), or a somewhat more direct and factual one from Heisenberg: "The mathematical formulations (of physics) no longer depict Nature, but rather our knowledge of Nature"(Heisenberg, 1955, p. 19).

If science can no longer be said to observe, explore, and eventually explain a "real" world, supposed to exist and to *be* the way it is, regardless of whether we are experiencing it or not, what then is science doing? "What science deals with is an *imagined* world" and it is "a construct, and some of the peculiarities of scientific thought become more intelligible when this fact is recognized" (Hebb, 1975, pp. 4 and 9). Scientists look for repetitive conjunctions among experiential (or experimental) data in the hope of establishing relatively reliable correlations or, better still, causal connections. They look for regularities in their experience that would allow the formulation of rules that could then be used, in the same old inductive fashion, to explain past experiences and to predict future ones.

In short, scientists seem to be involved in a process of learning that, *qua* process, is not at all unlike the learning of our ultrasimple model organism. Instead of establishing experiential regularities from which to derive rules of action to eliminate disturbances, they are searching for experiential regularities from which to derive rules of conceptualization for a homogeneous, internally consistent ordering of experience. In doing this, they encounter no shortage of disturbances that, as in the simple feedback model, must be eliminated. But the disturbances are now created by incompatibilities of rules and conceptualizations. And a closer look at the history of science should convince anyone that scientists, in their quest for consistency and compatibility, are prepared not only to modify the conceptual relations by means of which they order experiential items, but also to restructure quite radically those items that they consider basic elements (see Hanson, 1958; Kuhn, 1970; Feyerabend, 1975).

The Use of Black Boxes

One of the early contributions of cybernetics to the theory

of scientific analysis and investigation was the concept of a black box. It is obviously and exclusively an observer's concept. It is used for items that one suspects of performing some function, but that, for one reason or another, one cannot dismantle to see what is going on inside. Thus one might say, black boxes do not exist, but there may be many boxes that are black for someone. Living organisms are a case in point, especially the functions that, one suspects, constitute their intelligence. When one cuts open the organism, most of its interesting functions remain invisible or have ceased.

Cyberneticists in general, unlike the strict behaviorists who profess no interest in the internal machinery of a black box, are ready to make conjectures and to test their plausibility, much as scientists in other fields formulate and test hypotheses about things not directly observable. But there is one important difference. Other scientists believe that sooner or later they will be able to match their hypotheses with the real thing and find out whether they were right or wrong. A true cyberneticist knows that the "intelligent" functions he is investigating are never observable. All he can possibly check on is the material they start with and the results they produce: their *input* and *output*. Hence he tries to design a model that, given the same input, will always produce the same output as the black box. Although it is rewarding to design a physical model that actually works, cyberneticists much more often (for practical reasons or for lack of time or money) have to be satisfied with theoretical models that demonstrate at least that there is a logically feasible way of performing the function.

There are two aspects of the study of cognitive development that warrant the use of the black box concept. The first might seem almost trivial, if it were not for the widespread misunderstandings that certain models of cognitive development have generated. For the observing psychologist, the developing child is in many ways a very black box. But the observer, when he hypothesizes the child's intelligent or cognitive processes, must try to adopt a perspective *from inside the black box*. To say that he must try to see things from the child's point of view is to say far too little. It is *not* a

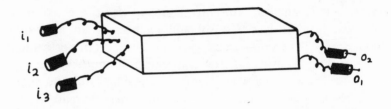

Figure 1. An item is considered a "black box" if, for one reason or another, the observer cannot investigate what goes on inside it. All he can see are inputs (i_1, i_2, i_3, . . .) and outputs (o_1, o_2, . . .). On the basis of continued observation, both the behaviorist and the cyberneticist will attempt to establish regularities in the input-output sequences. If this can be achieved, the behaviorist is satisfied because the observed regularities allow him to make certain probabilistic predictions about the item's behavior. The cyberneticist goes on to ask what kind of mechanism *inside* the box could account for the observed regularities. Hence he will try to construct a "model" that produces the same input-output sequences as the black box.

question of trying to see the same things the observer sees but from a different angle. Instead, it is a question of hypothesizing how such a black box, whose cognitive processor has access to nothing but proximal data, or internal events, can possibly articulate and structure its experiential field to end up with a viable representation of an "external" world.

So the naive realist view, that what we experience has to be a more or less direct reflection of an independently existing reality in which everything is fully structured and fixed, has made insight into cognitive development impossible. On that basis, development seems an obligatory one-way street of maturation and learning—in the sense of "finding out" or "discovering" how things really are and how they work. The only theoretical puzzle would be that development so rarely leads to any adequate understanding or wisdom.

This leads to the second use I want to suggest for the black-box concept. If it is the experiencer's intelligence or cognitive activity that, by organizing itself, organizes his experience into a viable representation of a world, then one can consider that representation a model, and the "outside reality" it claims to represent, a black box. The moment we

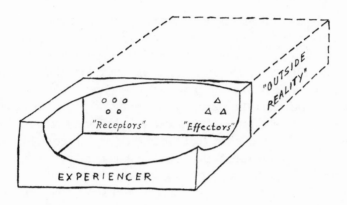

Figure 2. From the experiencer's point of view, "experience" basically consists of signals, which he may divide into "receptor" and "effector" or "sensory" and "motor" signals. His representation of an "outside reality" will necessarily be based on such regularities as he can establish in the experienced signal sequences. He has no way of investigating the "outside" except by observing what sensory signals follow upon certain effector signals which he has categorized as "activities." Hence his representation of the outside reality will be a model of an inaccessible black box in which the input, which he registers as effector signals, is systematically related to the output, which he registers as receptor signals.

attribute to the learning homeostat (to use our original example) the capabilities of representation and hypothesis, it can begin to conjecture how it comes about that a certain activity regularly results in the modification of a certain sensory signal. It can begin to construct a representation of an orderly external world with which it has two conceivable points of contact: "input" in the form of its effect on the outside, and "output" in the form of outside events that cause its own sensory signals. The representation, therefore, will have to be no more and no less than a hypothetical model of functions, entities, and events that could "explain" regularities in the organism's experience. And as a cyberneticist would expect, there is no way to match the model against the "real" structure of the black box.

Observer and Observed

To observe means to focus attention with particular care. When we use the verb transitively (which we usually do), it implies that a particular area of our experiential field is discriminable from the rest. Logically speaking, that part of our experience is the object we are observing. Psychologists, however, persistently speak of observing *subjects*. There are two reasons for that practice. First, psychologists presumably want to indicate at once that what they are observing is not a dead object but an active item that can play the role of subject in a number of activities. For the rigid behaviorist, of course, this is merely a conventional and somewhat misleading manner of speech, because in his view the rats he runs would be as passively determined by outside events as billiard balls or any other mindless objects. The cognitive psychologist, on the other hand, is ready to attribute subject-properties and even subjectivity to the items on which he focuses his attention. In other words, he deliberately looks for cognitive organization and cognitive functions.

The second reason psychologists say they observe subjects is that they do not want to acknowledge their own activity as observers. By calling the observed item "subject," they hide the fact that it is their own observer's activity that determines the items they observe.

Usually, to *observe* comprises a little more than just focusing attention on discriminable items. It also involves an attempt to isolate some form of interaction between the part of the observer's experience that he considers to be an organism and the rest of his experiential field, which he now considers that organism's environment.

In principle, this division between organism and environment is quite similar to the figure-ground division an artist makes when he draws the outline of an object on a sheet of paper. The point is this: just as the artist's figure and ground are both parts of the sheet of paper, so the organism and its environment are parts of the observer's field of experience. There can be no doubt that the division between an observed organism and its environment is both legitimate and extremely useful, provided we remain aware of who makes the division and where it is made (von Foerster, 1970). This awareness alone can help us to avoid two traps that have generated enormous confusion in the past.

First, there is the tempting but logically erroneous idea that what we rightly call "environment" relative to an organism when both the organism *and* its environment are being observed by us, must also be our environment and can, therefore, be held causally responsible for what we ourselves experience. Second, there is the mistaken belief that that "environment" which is part of *our* experiential field has to be identical with the experiential field of the observed organism (von Glasersfeld, 1976).

The conception of an experiencer who, facing a black-box reality, constructs a model of a world out of such regularities as he can establish in his experience provides us with a new perspective on some of the age-old problems of traditional epistemology. Similarly, the conception of an observer observing organisms that for him are black boxes with their own inaccessible fields of experience, provides a perspective on the study of cognitive development that only a few psychologists and educators have begun to appreciate. Among those few, of course, looms Piaget. The next section deals with his analysis of some of the most fundamental cognitive constructs.

PIAGET FROM A CYBERNETIC VIEWPOINT

The Construction of Permanent Objects

One of the revolutionary findings of Piaget's research in cognitive development was that it takes the child almost all of his first two years to acquire the notion that objects have an "existence" of their own and can be presumed, under ordinary circumstances, to remain what they are, even when one is not actually perceiving them. The discovery was revolutionary because in our adult, common-sense world there is probably not a single everyday thought or activity that does not in some crucial way rely upon that notion of object permanence. It is perhaps the most deeply rooted notion after that of our own existence. Most of us, failing after a long, meticulous search to find a misplaced object, would doubt our wife's, husband's or dearest friend's honesty, rather than give up the belief that the object must be *somewhere*. Hence it is quite a shock to be told that as children we did not start out with that notion but gradually and laboriously acquired it.

Piaget's analysis of that acquisition, the six stages into which he has articulated it, and the observational and experimental documentation he and others have accumulated during 50 years of research are well known. So, taking for granted that children can and do develop a concept of object permanence, I shall briefly examine some of the steps that seem indispensable for a hypothetical model of an organism to construct a similar concept.

There is hardly an introductory text of psychology today that does not refer to the child's development of the concept of object permanence. Looking at some of them, however, one gets the impression that the authors never read beyond the first hundred pages of Piaget's *The Construction of Reality in the Child* (1937/1971). In that first section of the book he does, of course, expound his theory of the genesis of the object concept, while the subsequent sections deal with the concepts of space, causality, time, and, finally, the universe. Though he treats the construction of these concepts sequentially, he makes it very clear that he does not consider them sequential in the child's development. In his view, one conceptual construction gives rise to all these concepts. In other words, experiential objects, space, causality, time—and I would add the concepts of change, motion, substance, identity, and self—all stem from *one* common initial construction and are therefore *connate* and inextricably interrelated. Hence, mention of "steps" in subsequent paragraphs does not imply a chronological but a logical sequence. There are certain steps that are logically indispensable prerequisites for others. But the logic is our logic, an *observer's* logic, and as such it applies to a model the observer is building.

Establishing "Sameness"

Before anything like the notion of permanence can arise,

there must be the possibility of separating items in experience and, then, of considering them the same. Some such ability, clearly, would be a prerequisite in any organism that operates inductively—that establishes recurrences in its experience, considers them regularities, and draws inferences from them. Indeed, there could be no learning at all if there were not some notion of sameness. For the behaviorist, of course, it is simply a basic fact that organisms are capable of "stimulus generalization." Taking the ability for granted helps in avoiding theoretical problems, but not in constructing a viable model of organisms and their behavior. In our inquiry, to which the concepts of recurrence, regularity, and permanence are indispensable, we cannot avoid asking how an organism could act as though two experiences were *the same.*

Even if we wanted to believe that perception is nothing but an organism's internal replication of a ready-made external world in which objects are *given,* we would have to explain how such an internal replication is constituted. This question runs into the same difficulty regardless of whether it is asked by a realist or by a constructivist. Neither can disregard the simple fact that an "object," from the point of view of the experiencing organism (i.e., in terms of the organism's sensory experience) is never quite the same on different occasions.

For example, the visual experience that we consider an instance of a specific object is different every time. The object's shape changes according to the angle, and its size according to the distance, from which it is seen. Its color changes according to the illumination, and other parameters are no less variable according to changes in the context. What, then, constitutes the invariant object which the organism recognizes? There seems to be no way around the assumption that, as far as the organism is concerned, an "object" must be a construct, actively abstracted from a number of experiences by holding on to a somewhat flexible constellation of characteristics and allowing each of them to vary within a certain range.

A closely related problem is that of the child's acquisition of names. Most psycholinguists agree that the child has to form some kind of concept before he can learn to associate a name with it, but there are different ideas on how that concept develops. Roger Brown (1958) summarized the two extremes and then provided a convincing synthesis.

> Suppose a very young child applies the word *dog* to every four-legged creature he sees. He may have abstracted a limited set of attributes and created a large category, but his abstraction will not show up in his vocabulary. Parents will not provide him with a conventional name for his category, e.g. *quadruped*, but instead will require him to narrow his use of *dog* to its proper range. . . .
>
> The child who spontaneously hits on the category four-legged animals will be required to give it up in favor of dogs, cats, horses, cows, and the like. . . . The schoolboy who learns the word *quadruped* has abstracted from differentiated and named subordinates. The child he was abstracted through a failure to differentiate. Abstraction after differentiation may be the mature process, and abstraction from a failure to differentiate the primitive.

Categorizing experiential objects in the particular way prescribed by the language the child has to acquire is, of course, not quite the same as deriving an object-concept from two or more experiences (see section on "Equivalence and Continuity"). But in both cases differentiation and abstraction seem to play much the same role. In the naming of objects it is the conventional nature of linguistic expressions that compels the child to structure his concepts in a certain way. In the construction of recursively usable object-concepts it is the organism's active search for recurrence and regularity that compels it to create "sameness" by focusing on similarities and disregarding differences. In Piagetian terms, this active imposition of invariance on instances of experience that are always different in some way, is the ubiquitous process of *assimilation.*

Assimilation and Accommodation

In the last paragraph I tried to show that an object-concept can only be the result of the experiencing organism's active construction. Even if an observer with realist convictions believes that the object is a ready-made "thing-in-itself" out there in reality waiting to be experienced, for an organism, every single experience of that object would nevertheless be a little different. So there is no immediate way of justifying the assumption that the concept of such an object could be a directly derived replica or representation of the "real" thing.

Giving up the realist epistemology, however, does not solve all problems. There remains, above all, the practical question how an organism could recognize an experience as the repetition of a previous one, when the two experiences are, in fact, not congruent in the sensory or experiential elements that compose them.

Piaget has resolved this difficulty by the introduction of the concept of *assimilation.* "To assimilate" means literally to make *like,* and Piaget uses the term quite literally.

> At the beginnings of assimilatory activity, any object whatever presented by the external environment to the subject's activity is simply something to suck, to look at, or to grasp.
>
> In its beginnings, assimilation is essentially the utilization of the external environment by the subject to nourish his hereditary or acquired schemata (Piaget, 1971, pp. ix and 396).

As observers, we may legitimately speak of the organism and its "external environment," but the organism cannot make that distinction with regard to itself, it merely has its own experience. Hence, from the organism's point of view, to assimilate means to modify a present experience so that it fits a hereditary or acquired schema, i.e., a perceptual or motor pattern that already has, in some sense, the character of an invariant. In other words, invariants create repetition as much as repetition creates invariants. This may not be nearly as paradoxical as it sounds. The linguistic example of names may once more help to illuminate the point. Having established four-leggedness as the invariant criterial feature of the complex experience associated with the word *dog,* the child focuses on four-leggedness and uses the word *dog* whenever that feature is available among the experiential material. That means that the child will *assimilate* all sorts of items—many of which he would later call *cat, horse, sheep,* or *cow*—and in doing so, he will disregard all the experiential elements that might distinguish them from the original experience associated with the word *dog*.

Needless to say, this is an extreme simplification. To my knowledge no child has ever assimilated a chair, a sofa, or a kitchen table to the concept named *dog*, and that should alert us to the fact that the child's concept of dog, by the time he begins to name things, must involve more criterial features than just four-leggedness. However, the principle is useful, and it helps us visualize not only how over-extension of a word or concept can develop, but also how the child eventually reduces it. As Brown pointed out, parents will require the child to narrow his use of *dog* to its proper range. That is, the child's misuse of dog will create disturbances in his experience, so there will be unexpected sequels to the use of the word. Such negative feedback can be eliminated only by a modified use of the word, i.e., by its restriction.

In Piagetian terms, such a reduction of over-extension is a case of accommodation. Assimilation, we have said, is the application of an established invariant pattern or schema to a present experience regardless of discrepancies. In accommodation, on the other hand, a discrepancy leads to the formation of a new pattern (either a modification of an old one or a novel assembly) that may then become a new invariant. The question that immediately arises is this: why should a discrepancy in experience sometimes lead to accommodation, and thus to the creation of a new schema, and at other times, in assimilation, be disregarded? The answer is not too difficult, provided we view the organism as a fundamentally goal-directed system.

Piaget suggests this frequently by saying that the organism must be considered an active experiencer rather than a passive receiver of stimuli. In the excerpts quoted above, he is even more specific: the organism assimilates items *in order to* suck, look at, or grasp. These activities, like all others which the organism has or acquires, have a certain sequential pattern and usually lead to certain experiential results. They are procedures toward certain experiential goals. But to be attained, these goals require the support (i.e., the presence) of more or less specific elements of experience. And there may be occasions when the elements present could not be assimilated to conform to the expected results of the activity.

When an infant, for instance, assimilates some visual elements to the invariant pattern that, for him, constitutes a rattle, and grasps and shakes a piece of wood that happens to be within reach, then the absence of the auditory element expected to ensue may cause a discrepancy that cannot be eliminated by assimilation. In that case, attention is likely to be focused on any of the formerly disregarded visual or tactual elements by means of which the piece of wood could be discriminated from the rattle. Once the discrimination has occurred, the new elements, with or without some of the old ones, can be associated in an act of *accommodation* to form a novel schema. This novel schema, from then on, will serve as a relatively independent invariant for the assimilation of future experiences.

I hope this brief exposition of the complex interaction of assimilatory and accommodatory processes has indicated that this part of Piaget's theory is compatible with the cybernetic approach. To refer once more to the feedback model, one might say that assimilation, insofar as it adjusts sensory signals, reduces the generation of error signals. Accommodation, on the other hand, occurs only when there is a discrepancy or disturbance for which the organism does not yet have an established remedy.

Schemas and Conceptual Structures

In discussing the role of assimilation in the generation of "sameness," and that of accommodation in the generation of invariants, I have referred to "elements of experience" as though these elements were always perceptual data. That was an extreme simplification.

"The object is in the first instance only known through the subject's actions, and therefore must be itself constructed" (Piaget, 1972, p. 82). For Piaget, early instances of "objects" are always subsections of an action schema. They are the sensory schemas which, in conjunction with a motor schema, constitute a sensory-motor activity. As such they are always a compound of perceptual as well as proprioceptive data. That is to say, they are a schema composed not only of several sensory signals but also of signals in several sensory modes. Usually this means that they contain visual and tactual signals as well as proprioceptive signals deriving from the motor activity of the perceiver.

As the result of many acts of accommodation that added or removed particular experiential elements, an object-schema becomes relatively invariant and may be used to assimilate new experience. But all this still takes place on the level of sensory-motor activities and, though it may serve as partial model for later developments, it does not entail the formation of concepts. Hence this use of an invariant schema is by no means a manifestation of the concept of object permanence, because its invariance arises from and consists in the repetition of an activity and does not yet involve the invariance of an independent object.

> The growth of the human mind partly consists of the successive attainment or formation of cognitive *invariants*. As its name suggests, an invariant is something that remains the same while other things in the situation change or undergo various transformations. The identification of constant features or invariants in the midst of flux and change is an absolutely indispensable cognitive activity for an adaptive organism, and it is particularly characteristic of human rationality (Flavell, 1977, p. 48).

Cognitive invariants may often have the same content as invariant sensory or motor schemas, but we attribute to them an additional feature that takes them out of the world of sensory-motor experience: we assume that they are available to the organism regardless of the sensory signals at the moment. They constitute part of the material on a second level of experience that is made possible by memory, a level of experience that we call *representation* to differentiate it from the level of perception and proprioception.

Introspectively we *know* that we can operate on a representational level. Empirically we know that people can solve quite complicated problems in their heads (i.e., without perceptual crutches, such as pencil and paper) and that some of them can even play several games of chess simultaneously without any visual aids whatever. Nevertheless I do not want to say that adults or children have representations as a matter of fact. All I intend is that the kind of model a cognitivist constructs to "explain" the functioning of such organisms must have that capability.

Once a system is equipped with this ability to maintain experiential compounds invariant and to use them independently of present sensory experience, all sorts of interesting things become possible. For the moment I shall mention only two. First, the term *invariant* acquires a new dimension. In the context of sensory-motor assimilation, it was always a perceptual or motor activity that was called invariant because it did not change in the face of different sensory material. Now, if the invariant can be used on the representational level, without an activity, it becomes like a program or a subroutine that is invariant in that it is stored somewhere in a memory from which it can be retrieved. It is this change of status that gives rise to the concepts of permanence and of *identity*, a further step in the construction of permanent objects.

The second development made possible by the introduction of the representational use of invariants is that they can now be used as building blocks for conceptual constructions that move further and further away from the raw material of sensory or motor signals. This shift constitutes one of the salient characteristics of all the "higher," more sophisticated mental operations and it has consequences for epistemology far beyond the scope of this essay. But, the principle of (1) learning to construct a composite in a certain way and out of certain elements, (2) storing the program or recipe of construction, and (3) retrieving it as a unit to combine with others of parallel origin and form a "higher-level" structure, *without* having to return to the "lower" level, has proven to be one of the most powerful in the construction of knowledge. It allows us to proceed much as a bricklayer, who can devote all his energy and attention to the creation of a wall or an arch, without ever stopping to ask where the bricks he is using came from and how they were made. And just as the characteristics of the bricks (e.g., shape and size) make it impossible for the bricklayer to build certain structures, so the ready-made conceptual building blocks impose constraints on any future construction.

The Ambiguity of "Sameness"

In everyday situations, when we say that an item *is the same*, we know what we mean and we are rarely misunderstood. If two or more items are present, there is no problem. We are saying that, in a way usually defined by context, we find no difference between the items and therefore consider them *equivalent.* If, however, only the one item is within our actual field or experience, the expression is ambiguous. It may be interpreted again as an assertion of equivalence, but it may also be interpreted as asserting that the present item is the *selfsame* individual that we have encountered at some other time.

The same ambiguity is inherent in the everyday use of the word *identical.* Although English provides a logically impeccable way of distinguishing the two meanings by the use of a different article (*an identical one* for equivalence, *the identical one* for individual identity), they are frequently interchanged in ordinary usage. As long as we are referring to fairly familiar items, this does not seem to lead to confusion.

In a discussion of conceptual invariants, however, the ambiguity of "sameness" and "identity" becomes a serious obstacle to understanding. Indeed, if we want to grasp the concept of object permanence, it is indispensable that we completely resolve that ambiguity.

Earlier, we asked the question "What constitutes the invariant object that the organism *recognizes?*" If we take this question without context, "invariant" clearly could be interpreted in two radically different ways. On the one hand, it could be a prototype, or template, by which the organism categorizes certain experiences as exemplars of the class represented by the invariant. This is the sense of *object concept* and it was then illustrated by the example from psycholinguistics. On the other hand, the "invariant" could be interpreted as an object in its own right that remains unchanged because it "exists" and is recognized as the *selfsame* individual everytime it enters the organism's field of experience. This is the sense of "invariant" that corresponds to the conception of *object permanence.* Both the concept of the object as prototype, with regard to which experiences may be considered equivalent, and the concept of object permanence, as a result of which two or more experiences may be considered to derive from one identical individual, involve a form of invariance. But the invariance is certainly not the same in both cases. William James, who had an exceptionally keen eye for conceptual distinctions, said seventy years ago,

> Permanent "things" again; the "same" thing and its various "appearances" and "alterations"; the different "kinds" of thing . . . it is only the smallest part of his experience's flux that anyone actually does straighten out by applying to it these conceptual instruments. Out of them all our lowest ancestors probably used only, and then most vaguely and inaccurately, the notion of "the same again." But even then if you had asked them whether the same were a "thing" that had endured throughout the unseen interval, they would probably have been at a loss, and would have said that they had never asked that question, or considered matters in that light (James, 1907/1955, p. 119).

In this very limited, specific, but important respect, much of the literature on objects, identity, and the concept of self still seems to avoid that question and to shirk "considering matters in that light."

Equivalence and Continuity

The process of assimilation discussed earlier leads to practical, action-bound implementations of the notion of "the same again" in that it actively shapes a present experience to fit an available sensory-motor schema. At that level one could speak of object-*schemas.* The term object-*concept,* however, should be reserved for constructs on the representational level, i.e., constructs that can be called up regardless of the sensory elements that are or are not available at the moment. If we accept this distinction (and if we want to attribute cognitive processes and operations to an organism, we must accept it), then also the *concepts* of recurrence, sameness, identity, and permanence will have to be constructed on the representational level. An attempt to map this construction in detail seems out of the question at present, but we can, I believe, outline some of the major steps.

No recurrence can possibly be established unless there are records of past experiences and the possibility of surveying them in some way. That requires not only memory and retrieval capabilities (which I shall take for granted), but that the experiencing organism can switch his attention from "present" items to the records of "past" items. It is only by switching from one item to another that absence of difference can be established, with the result that the two experiential items are the same. Eliane Vurpillot (1972) has elegantly documented the switching to and fro of children's eyes during visual comparison tasks. Eye movements indicate shifts of attention in the visual field. Shifts of attention, however, have also been observed when eye movement is eliminated by stabilizing the visual image (Pritchard, Heron, and Hebb, 1960; Zinchenko and Vergiles, 1972). Hence we may safely assume that attention can also shift between items when some or all of them are representational.

An analysis of the actual procedure of comparison also has conceptual implications. If the *direction* of comparison is from item *A* to item *B*, in the sense that the characteristics found in *A* are then checked in *B*, item *B* may be considered the same (in the likeness sense) if no difference is registered in the checked characteristics. But in that case *B* may or may not have characteristics which are not represented at all in *A*. Hence it should not be called "equivalent," let alone "identical." In order to establish *equivalence*, the comparison would have to be carried out in both directions. This distinction is of considerable practical importance, since it is all too easy to overlook the fact that in classifying or categorizing, as a rule, a one-directional comparison is all that is made.

The direction of the comparison in classification, clearly, is from a representational prototype, or concept, to an experiential item. The nature of the class depends on precisely those characteristics that have been abstracted and combined to form the concept. (This could again be illustrated by the example of the child that abstracts, say, four-leggedness and spontaneous motion to form a concept and then—erroneously, from the adult point of view—associates the word *dog* with that concept.)

The procedural analysis also helps to throw some light on the still mysterious ambiguity of "sameness." To establish that two experiential items are equivalent, the simplest and most reliable way is to arrange them side by side in our visual field.[1] We can then switch our attention from one to the other and check out all the characteristics we consider relevant. This is precisely what Vurpillot demonstrated in her study, and she also noted the one peculiar feature in the procedure. "By convention, one difference is always excluded from the list of properties [to be compared] and that is the object's location relative to the subject. Since they [the objects] can never appear at the same place at the same time, they will always be different from that point of view" (Vurpillot, 1972, p. 311; my translation).

In other words, when we say that two items are "equivalent in every respect," we understand that "in every respect" does not include spatial location. It is also clear that we accept the fact that the two items do *not* "appear at the same place at the same time" as evidence that they are not one and the same individual, even if we can find no other difference between them. This, I think, brings out very clearly the difference between the two meanings of "sameness." The construct of equivalence involves two experiential items and comparison of a set of properties that does not yield a difference. Ideally, we have both items in our field of experience, separate but in a way that allows us to shift our attention from one to the other in *both* directions.[2] But if this ideal cannot be achieved, because for some reason it is impossible to have both items in the experiential field, we may suspect that we are dealing with one individual only. There is, indeed, no foolproof way of ascertaining that this is not the case. That raises the question of how we can consider two experiential items as one, even when they are separated by other experiences.

At the core of this problem of individual identity is the conception of continuity. As long as an item remains within our field of vision and is marginally attended to, there is no problem. Continuity is the uninterrupted succession of signals from one source. If the item is a composite of signals from different sources, each of them will be constantly available to attention (which is *not* the case with alternating lights and, therefore, leads to the phi phenomenon; see note 2 at the end of this chapter).

But consider a case in which there is no continuous succession at all but, nevertheless, we are able to construe individual identity. A well-fed brother whom one has not seen for twenty years may be bald and scrawny when he returns; he may have a different accent, his likes and dislikes may have changed, and what he now says about politics, art, and women may be incompatible with what one remembers of him. Yet one could still accept him as the selfsame individual. How do we construct continuity across such enormous experiential gaps? I believe we acquire the ability in small steps.

The first step is to assume continuity of a composite whole on the strength of an experientially continuous part. We do this every time we watch a moving object that for a moment partially disappears and then comes into full sight again. In an infant's early life, that is a frequent experience since there are nearly always some visual obstacles in the immediate environment behind which parts of people disappear. Visual tracking is manifest very early and soon enables the infant to follow an item even when it wholly disappears for a moment (Bower, 1974). In that case it cannot be a visual part of the experiential item, but rather the proprioceptive signals generated by the tracking motion that supply the continuity. The essential feature, however, is the experiential continuity of *some* signal sequence that connects the percept that disappears with the percept that reappears, and that can hold the child's attention so no other item comes into focus. If there is no such sequence and, consequently, there is a refocusing of attention in the interval, the two experiential items will not be construed as one individual, no matter how similar they may be as percepts. For many five-year-olds, for instance, the sun today and the sun yesterday are not yet one and the same individual (Piaget, 1971, p. 87).

As long as the linear sequence of attention focused on sensory signals is the only dimension of the child's experience, it is logically impossible to connect two experiential items across an interval during which *none* of the signals constituting them is continuous. Such a connection has to be created *outside* the ongoing experiential sequence, so that it can subsist, as it were, in parallel and is not broken by the actual sensory experiences that occur during the interval. This second dimension is the representational one, and hand in hand with its development goes the process that Piaget has called *externalization*. He speaks of a "miniature Copernican revolution" at the end of the sensory-motor period, as a result of which the child begins to see himself as a permanent object among other permanent objects "in a universe that he has gradually constructed himself, and which hereafter he will experience as external to himself" (Piaget, 1967, p. 9).

It is easy to see that this externalization of items has a momentous effect on the way we thenceforward think and speak of experience and knowledge. It accomplishes a conceptual revolution that is almost impossible to *undo*. Perhaps the most remarkable thing is that the logical analysis that inexorably reduces regularities and continuity in our experience to our own constructive activities comes to a halt in the case of the returning brother. For if we do accept him as the selfsame individual who left twenty years ago, it is not on the basis of equivalences we establish on the level of immediate sensory experience, but only because he is able to recollect and communicate particular experiential items, such as objects, situations, and events, that the person of twenty years ago had occasion to construct. His individual identity, in the last analysis, depends not on the permanence of what we usually call physical characteristics, but on the permanence of his recollections or, if you will, his mind.

The Problem of Reality

The outside realm into which we place items *as we repre-*

sent them to ourselves when we are *not* experiencing them—a kind of limbo where ready-made objects await entry into the process of our assimilatory experience—inevitably turns into what philosophers call "ontological reality." As soon as we conceive of continuity as an inherent property of things, we have laid the foundation for a world that "exists," a world that is "there" whether we happen to perceive it or not, a world that, ultimately, is wholly detached from the experiencing subject.

Instead of becoming aware of ourselves as creators of continuity and thus of recurrence and regularity in the flow of our proximal signals, we begin to attribute continuity and permanence to our constructs. They become an independent distal "reality," and our acts of experience take on the character of exploration and discovery of things that are already there quite apart from ourselves. As a result of our detachment we find ourselves facing that most peculiar, unanswerable question of traditional epistemology—how we, irrevocably tied to our ways and means of experiencing, can ever transcend that limitation and acquire "true knowledge of the real world."

Some Basic Constructs

The preceding pages have laid out some implications of Piaget's theory of early cognitive development that are rarely emphasized because they require a rather drastic modification of our common-sense ideas. To conclude this section, I shall try to indicate very briefly how some of the concepts indispensable in our construction of reality derive from the basic assumptions in this early development.

Space. The early continuity the child constructs, for example, on the basis of his own tracking motion, is the continuity of a schema and does not involve a conception of the disappearing object continuing its path behind the visual obstacle. Once that conception is formed by externalizing a representation, however, the external permanent object requires a place, somewhere *beyond* the experiential field, where it can "exist" when it is not being experienced. Such a place, before it is particularized by spatial relationships to other items or to the experiencer, constitutes the basic concept of *space*. Its one and only feature is that it allows an arrangement of perceptual items such that *attention can shift from one to the other in both directions and at the discretion of the perceiver.* When this shift of attention is actually carried out in perception, it is accompanied by proprioceptive signals from eyes, hand, or some other part of the body (indicating what an observer would call "motion") and this addition of signals leads to the concept of *extension*.

Change. Once the continuity of an item is established by means of an experientially continuous part or through the continuity of related proprioceptive signals, a comparison of all the characteristics of the present item with those of the record of the time from before the interval may yield a difference. If we then want to maintain the item as a continuous one, we shall consider it *changed* but, nevertheless, the same individual. The more characteristics are changed, the more difficult it becomes to maintain the continuity of the individual, and we are driven to anchor the continuity in more and more abstract (i.e., less sensory) characteristics. An ice cube that has melted, or a log that has turned to ashes in the fireplace, tax our conception of continuity. In cases where there is even less to hold on to, we try to make do, as did Aristotle, with the paradoxical construct of "substance," which supports individuality without having itself any properties at all. The search for this mysterious substance must forever fail because, having no properties, it cannot be found on the level of sensory signals.

Motion. A very particular kind of change is the one that involves not a characteristic of the permanent object itself, but some relationship with another item in the experiential field. According to whether relationships (e.g., inclusion, contiguity, proximity) are being terminated, maintained, or newly established, we get *change of location* or *change of extension* of the object. Any repetitive change that involves the forming and ending of relationships with a succession of different items will be considered some form of *motion*.

Since the origin of these concepts is under all circumstances a change of relationships, the attribution of motion to a particular item always requires a further point of reference or other sensory signals.

Cause. When there is change and we explicitly register a difference between the two experiences, it is obviously more difficult to maintain the item's individual identity than if there is no change. Indeed, we are construing the two experiences as one individual on the one hand and as different on the other. I believe it is this apparent clash which later drives us to search so persistently for causal explanations.

The practice of causation originates with the infant's "circular reactions" (Piaget, 1971, p. 351), the *instrumental* repetition of certain actions because they have, in the past, led to satisfying consequences. The infant shakes the hand holding the rattle because this has been followed by somehow pleasing sensory signals. Similarly, the infant learns to pull a cloth in order to bring an object that is on it within reach. Once some of the sensory compounds involved in these situations have been externalized as permanent objects, the pleasing events can be seen as *changes* and the activity that regularly precedes such a change can be conceived as causing the change. On the conceptual level, then, once a cause is found, the clash between the maintained identity and the registered change is neutralized, because the change noted in the second experience can now be balanced by the cause as adjunct to the first experience. From there to the general conception that every change can be reduced to *some* cause, and that this cause need not be an activity of the experiencer, does not seem a very great step.

Time. The earlier statement that continuity derives from a succession of sensory signals from one source was simplified by leaving out a difficult but important point: a succession of similar signals cannot be perceived as a sequence unless the experiencer's attention takes in something else *between* the signals. If there is no such break, the signals, because they are all the same, cannot constitute a plurality and will be registered as one. On the other hand, if attention is interrupted by a total shift to something else, the signal before the break and the one after it will be perceived as separate, and there will be no *sensory* basis for the conception of continuity. The answer to this problem lies in the possibility of marginal (or, perhaps, divided) attention. We know this in the visual field, where attention can dart to the periphery *without* motion (i.e., without the addition of proprioceptive signals) and we can experience it also tactually by keeping track (in a dark room, for example) of the edge of a table with one hand, while we mainly focus on exploring the table's surface with the other. That is to say, we can, in fact, operate in two channels.[3] *Continuity* and sequence, thus, both spring from the juxtaposition of two successions of signals that are separate in the experiential field but interrelated by attention; the one is continuous relative to the other, the other is sequential relative to the first.

The concept of *time* arises when the sequential items are mapped or projected on the continuous one. In order to construct the temporal dimension, indeed, we always need *two* processes—the ticking of the clock as one, and as the other the hum of the traffic, the glow of a light, or anything else that we experience as continuous. With the abstraction of our *self* as experiencer from the flow of experience we create the most continuous of all continuous items on which we can project any succession of experiential elements as a temporal sequence. But, as we shall see in the next section, this continuous self is destined to remain a purely conceptual construct that we cannot encounter on the sensory level.

THE CONSTRUCTION OF SELF

Self Observing Itself

The concept of "self" seems simple enough when we refer to it in an accustomed context and in ordinary language. As a rule people do not object if one makes statements such as "That's typical of James" or "Well, I can't help it, I *am* like that." Even the rather peculiar expressions "You are you" and "I am I" do not seem as peculiar as Gertrude Stein's "A rose is a rose." What we apparently have in mind when we make any such statement is the individual identity or continuity of a person. However, as soon as we attempt to analyze what precisely it is that constitutes the continuity of our "selves," we run into difficulties and get the impression that there is an ambiguity. The "self" seems to have several different aspects.

First of all, there is a self that is part of one's perceptual experience. In my visual field, for instance, I can easily discriminate my hand from the writing pad and table and from the pencil it is holding. I have no doubt that the hand is part of *me,* while the pad, the table, and the pencil are not.

Second, if I move my eyes, tilt my head, or walk to the window, I can isolate my "self" as the locus of the perceptual (and other) experiences I am having. This self as the "experiencer" appears to be an active agent rather than a passive entity. It *can,* in fact, move my eyes, tilt my head, change location—and it can also attend to one part of the visual or experiential field rather than to another. This active self can decide to look or not to look, to move or not to move, to hold the pencil or not to hold it, and, within certain limits, to experience or not to experience.[4]

Beyond these, there are still other aspects of the concept of "self." There is, for instance, the *social* self: *qua* experiencers, we enter into specific relations to other experiencers, and *qua* actors, we adopt specific patterns or roles that eventually come to be considered characteristic parts of what we call our "selves." But this essay focuses on the early development of concepts, and I shall disregard the social aspects of the self because, although they, too, have some roots in the sensory-motor period, their main development seems to take place during adolescence.

In the paragraphs that follow, then, I shall be concerned exclusively with the self as perceptual entity and as experiencer.

The Self as Visual Percept

Perhaps the most serious obstacle that has impeded traditional psychology from arriving at a plausible analysis of the concept of "self" is the assumption that the dichotomy between an organism and its environment is basically the same as the dichotomy between an experiencing subject and what it experiences. As argued in the section "Observer and Observed," the distinction between an organism and its environment can be made only by an observer of the organism. The oganism itself has no access to distal data, to items outside itself. But with the construction of permanent objects the organism *externalizes* some of the invariants it abstracts from its experience and treats them, from then on, as independent external items. (See "Equivalence and Continuity" section.) This externalization, as we have seen, goes hand in hand with the establishing of *internal* representations or concepts, and this dual development of objects, which are "perceptual," and concepts, which are "representational," leads to a sharp division between two forms of experience, one "external" and the other "internal." (There are, of course, illusions, dreams, and hallucinations that, from the subject's point of view, blur that division.) Both the internal and the external, however, are explicitly *experience,* and the division between them, therefore, is a division between two types of experience and *not* the division between an experiencing subject and the objects it experiences.

Wapner and Werner (1965, p. 10) are aware of the problem and speak of two "complementary notions," a holistic one and a polar one.

Our theoretical-experimental approach has focused on two characteristics of this relationship between one's own body and environmental objects.

First of all, we assume that there can be no perception of objects "out there" without a bodily framework, and, conversely, we assume that there can be no perception of the body-as-object without an environmental frame of reference. Thus, one basic feature of this "body:object" relationship pertains to the interaction constantly going on between them. The central notion here is that the appropriate unit to be dealt with is not the organism per se, but rather, the organism in its environmental context, this conceptualization, then, is that the variability or stability of the biological unit, "body:environment," reflects itself in body perception as well as in object perception.

Second, complementary to this holistic notion of the biological unit composed of body and environment is a feature which is seemingly in contradiction to it, viz., the feature of oppositeness, or separateness, or polarity between these two elements. Such oppositeness is characteristic of the normal adult insofar as he experiences the world and himself as standing in polar distinction to each other.

I have quoted the two authors at some length because they seem to be more aware than any others I have read of the experiential origin of the "body percept" but they still represent the general confusion between the organism's perception of its own body and the conception of the "self" as the locus of experience.

The first step that leads to that confusion is the failure to separate what *only an observer* of organisms can say about organisms and their environments from what an organism itself may say about its experience. (See "Observer and Observed" section.)

When I visually distinguish a hand from the writing pad and the table on which it lies, I carry out exactly the same kinds of operations as when I distinguish the coffee cup from the table on which it stands, or the picture from the wall on which it hangs, or the cardinal outside my window from the branch on which it happens to be perched and from the rest of the landscape. In all these cases I am recognizing certain objects to which I have attributed relative consistency (closure) and permanence. Having successfully externalized permanent objects, I am now experiencing them as parts of "distal reality." From the purely visual point of view, the operations by means of which I separate objects from the rest of the visual field or "ground" are always the same kind. And the observer's distinction between an organism and its environment is *normally* made in the visual field (which is not to say that such a distinction *could* not be made in the tactual mode). Thus, although we can visually distinguish birds, coffee cups, tables, and hands from the rest of the visual field and from one another, it seems clear that a naive organism (i.e., an organism such as an infant that does not yet have a great deal of intermodally coordinated experiences) cannot *visually* discriminate between *a* hand and his *own* hand.

Trevarthen et al. (1975) have shown that, contrary to previous assumptions, infants in the very early stages of reaching and grasping do *not* make use of visual feedback concerning the hand's position. This seems likely because it takes an infant some time to relate the visual image of the hand to the "self" that has the motor command over it.

If one accepts the conclusion that there are no a priori *visual* features that differentiate visual experience of one's own body from visual experience of other items, one is at once compelled to raise the question how that differentiation could be made. As we shall see, there are several levels on which the coordination of sensory signals yields invariants that contribute to the constitution of a "permanent" entity corresponding to what we may call our "body percept." Before surveying these levels, however, I want to emphasize once more that, no matter how successful our analysis of the body percept may be, it cannot possibly tell us anything about the "self:world polarity" mentioned by Wapner and Werner (see quotation above), because insofar as the perception of one's self is the result of perceptual experience, it belongs to the world that is being experienced and not to the experiencer.

Levels of Self-Perception

If the Piagetian approach to the notion of object permanence is a viable one, it should not surprise us that the notion of self as a constant perceptual entity cannot be derived from vision alone. According to that theory, permanent objects are the result of the coordination of signals from more than one sensory source.[5] Since the body percept obviously *does* achieve the status of permanent object, it must be multimodal, and the question now is: what kinds of signals and coordinations of signals would enable an organism to differentiate one permanent object—his own body—from all the other permanent objects that have been constructed and externalized?

The answer is extremely complex; there are many factors that contribute to the differentiation and isolation of the body percept. In this summary exposition I shall sketch out a few of the points that seem crucial. Such an analysis is necessarily made by an observer who can only hypothesize what goes on in the black box we call an observed organism. (See "The Use of Black Boxes" section.) The indispensable limitation of this hypothesizing is that the organism can operate only with its own proximal data, i.e., with signals that can be supposed to originate within it rather than with "information" originating in what from the observer's point of view is the organism's environment. I would also like to emphasize that this analysis is provisional and lays no claim to being definitive, let alone exhaustive.

One of the primary factors seems to be the experience that there is motor control over certain visual items. When a discriminable item moves partially across an organism's visual field and the organism follows it with its gaze, the organism can correlate certain visual signals with the proprioceptive signals from its own tracking motion (eye and head movements). If the visual item happens to be, say, the organism's own hand, another kind of signal can also be correlated with the visual and tracking signals, namely the proprioceptive signals generated by the active motion of the hand. This additional correlation can be used to discriminate moving objects that are parts of the organism's own body from objects that are not.

This very elementary distinction is, of course, strongly reinforced by the fact that the organism is able to generate and control (i.e., direct, speed up, stop, etc.) the motion of its own limbs. This particular coordination of motor control on the basis of visual feedback, for instance in hand movements of human infants, is a difficult task and, as a rule, is not mastered until an age of six or seven months (Bower, 1977).

There are various experiential phenomena that confound these basic coordinations. If the moving hand happens to hold an object, it must be discriminated from the hand on the basis of *other* factors, such as tactual signals from the fingers, because, for the coordination of visual and proprioceptive signals, the held object is initially indistinguishable from the hand. Once the organism has a certain amount of experience, it will be able to discriminate its hand from other items on the basis of visual signals alone. This ability, however, consists in recognizing the hand as the one categorized as its *own* by nonvisual means.

The interplay with tactual signals is presumably essential for the evolution of a primitive visual and proprioceptive schema of the body percept. Every contact with other items that gives rise to tactual signals is an indication of the limits of the body. The progressive coordination of these "contact signals" with the accompanying visual signals is, in fact, the essential element in the organism's mastery of locomotion and other motor skills (Held, 1965/1972).

Tactual signals are also involved in another aspect of the body percept's ontogenesis. When an organism touches some part of his body with his hand, tactual signals are generated on both sides of the point of contact. This allows the organism to distinguish with great reliability between touching other things and touching himself. If the touch is vigorous, it may even give rise to pain. Kittens chase, catch, and occasionally bite not only their mother's and littermates' tails but also their own. There is no question that they quickly learn to distinguish their own tail when it comes to biting, and to that extent they have a notion of "self."

Similarly, the baby that sucks his thumb as well as the nipple of mother or bottle already has the sensory material to make a distinction that will be a primary source for the construction of both the body percept and the concept of self. And the same could be said of the grooming behaviors that nonhuman primates apply to their companions and themselves.

One further situation involving tactual signals may well supply the operational prototype for construction of the concepts of motion and time, and the sensory model of the continuously experiencing self. In the paragraph on basic concepts I said that any repetitive change that involves the forming and ending of relationships with a succession of different items will be considered a form of *motion.* Under the heading *time,* I said that continuity and sequence both spring from the juxtaposition of two successions of signals that are

separate in the experiential field but interrelated by attention. The one is continuous relative to the other, the other is
sequential relative to the first. Take a finger of your right
hand and run it along your left forearm: The tactual signals
originating in your finger will be a homogeneous "continuous" succession because the receptors from which they come
remain the same; the tactual signals originating in your left
arm, instead, will constitute a sequence of different signals
because they come from different receptors. If you consider
this second set of signals as a sequence of different locations
with which your finger establishes and terminates contact,
you will conceive of your finger as *moving*. If you consider
them equivalent units linked into sequence by the continuous
signals from your finger, you will conceive of them as points
or "moments" in *time*. In this second case, the finger of your
right hand supplies what is perhaps the closest sensory-motor
analogy to the continuity of the experiencing subject that we
call our "self."

The Image in the Mirror

On a later and more sophisticated level, once tactual and
proprioceptive elements have contributed to a protoconcept
of his own body, the child will be capable of visual recognition of his own hand or limbs. This sets the stage for a considerably more complex experience of the physical self: the
child's recognition of his own shadow, his reflection on a
shiny surface, and his image in a looking glass.

Gallup (1977), in a survey of research on self-recognition
in primates, comes to the conclusion that only the great apes
have the ability to recognize their mirror image as their own.
Monkeys and, as many of us have observed in our homes, cats
and dogs quickly learn to discriminate their shadows, reflec-
tions, and mirror images from *other* moving objects or
animals, but do not appear to relate them in any way to
themselves.[6] The simple synchrony of movement between,
say, a paw and its shadow or reflection does not seem sufficient to establish the link. It may be that a causal connection
must be constructed from a deliberate motion to its reflected
counterpart, and that it is this connection which differentiates

the motion of a mirror image from the motion of another object or organism.

The child who stands in front of a looking glass, sticks out his tongue, and contorts his face into all sorts of grimaces gets a constant confirmation of this causal link. The mirror image is as obedient as his own limbs and can, thus, be integrated with the body percept, expanding it by providing visual access to otherwise invisible aspects. And like the body image it is a visual percept, an item that is experienced, not the item that does the experiencing. This central item, the experiencer himself, remains mysterious. Without ever perceiving it, we know that it is at the heart of whatever continuity or invariant we construct in our perceptual world. As teen-agers, at one time or another, many of us stood in front of a looking glass and wondered: where am I? It is a question we are still unable to answer when we are adults.

THE CYBERNETIC METAPHOR

Sketchy and incomplete though they are, I hope the preceding paragraphs have shown that there are several relatively independent sources from which facets of the self percept can be developed. Much remains to be worked out, above all, the detailed analysis of the process by which these facets become integrated to what we so strongly feel to be a unitary concept of our self. While we can work out a plausible model for the self as an entity of our sensory-motor world of experience, this model cannot throw any light on what we feel to be our self as *experiencing entity*. The reason lies in the very structure of our conception of knowledge. In the western tradition of science and rational explanation, knowledge by its very nature requires a dichotomy between the knower and the things he knows. In other words, we can come to know only what we consider to be in some sense separate from our knowing selves. By questioning something, by the very act of asking what it *is*, we have already set our self, the questioner, apart.

In the realist view, the self we perceive, by being perceived, becomes the object of a perceiving subject. In the constructivist view, the self we conceive is necessarily the product of an active subject that remains outside the construction. It may be a viable construct in that it appears compatible with *what* we experience, but it does not and cannot incorporate that primary act of constructing itself. Berger and Luckmann (1967, p. 50) express this very neatly:

> On the one hand, man *is* a body, in the same way that this may be said of every other animal organism. On the other hand, man *has* a body. That is, man experiences himself as an entity that is not identical with his body, but that, on the contrary, has that body at its disposal. In other words, man's experience of himself always hovers in a balance between being and having a body, a balance that must be redressed again and again.

The two aspects seem wholly incompatible. The paradox of the self experiencing itself, from the logician's point of view, is analogous to the paradox of self reference. The logical paradox has recently been approached with great success through a novel interpretation of the concept of recursion (Varela, 1976), and it is surely no accident that the very same concept of recursion has opened an equally novel path towards the logical interpretation of "permanent objects" (von Foerster, 1976). An exposition of the formal intricacies of these achievements would be beyond the scope of both this essay and my competence. One general point, however, brings this discussion back to the place where it began.

Even a very simple system that regulates itself by negative feedback (such as Philon's oil lamp of two dozen centuries ago) must be characterized not by a description of its component parts but by a description of their circular interaction. The essence of the system, its individual identity that perpetuates it, cannot be ascribed to any particular part or property, nor can it be located in a particular point. The identity of such a system resides exclusively in the invariant that is the result of mutually balanced changes. The characteristic feature of Philon's lamp is not that its burner always remains full, but rather the paradox that lowering the oil level causes the oil level to be raised.

As a metaphor—and I stress that it is intended as a metaphor—the concept of an invariant that arises out of mutually or cyclically balancing changes may help us to approach the concept of self. In cybernetics this metaphor is implemented in the "closed loop," the circular arrangement of feedback mechanisms that maintain a given value within certain limits. They work toward an invariant, but the invariant is achieved not by a steady resistance, the way a rock stands unmoved in the wind, but by compensation over time. Wherever we happen to look in a feedback loop, we find the present act pitted against the immediate past, but already on the way to being compensated itself by the immediate future. The invariant the system achieves can, therefore, never be found or frozen in a single element because, by its very nature, it consists in one or more relationships—and relationships are not *in* things but between them.

If the self, as I suggest, is a relational entity, it cannot have a locus in the world of experiential objects. It does not reside in the heart, as Aristotle thought, nor in the brain, as we tend to think today. It resides in no place at all, but merely manifests itself in the continuity of our acts of differentiating and relating and in the intuitive certainty we have that our experience is truly ours.

Notes

1. I am here limiting the discussion to the visual aspect, but it should be clear that it applies equally to all sensory modalities, singly or in combination.

2. Note that in the phi phenomenon, where two lights flash in quick alternation, the viewer's attention, though shifting in both directions, cannot do so at its own rate but is obliged to keep pace with the lights; this destroys the "twoness" and results in the perception of one *moving* light.

3. A manifestation of "parallel processing" in the auditory mode is found in musicians who in a fugue, for example, are perfectly able to keep track of two rhythmically different sequences. Of great interest in this regard is also the recent work on levels of awareness by Hilgard (1974).

4. While Oriental philosophy has always cultivated this autonomy of the experiencer, the Western world, in defense of its traditional belief in an objective reality, has tended to consider experience as obligatory, inevitable, and rather passive.

5. In accepting this view it is essential to realize that there are certain intermediary phenomena between the simple association of, say, visual signals on the basis of their contiguity, and the fully fledged schema of a permanent object composed of signals of multimodal origin. Permanent two-dimensional shapes, for instance, are the result of program-like patterns in which visual signals are linked by a continuous pathway of proprioceptive data or moments of attention. (See Ceccato, 1960; Shumaker, 1977; von Uexküll, 1933/ 1970.)

6. This must also be so for all wild animals, since they do not take fright when they lower their heads to drink from a water hole.

References

Ashby, W. Ross. 1970. Learning in a Homeostat. *Symposium on Artificial Intelligence.* Knoxville: University of Tennessee.

Berger, P. L., and Luckmann, T. 1966. *The Social Construction of Reality.* Garden City, N.Y.: Doubleday (Anchor paperback, 1967).

Bower, T.G.R. 1974. *Development in Infancy.* San Francisco: Freeman.

Bower, T.G.R. 1977. *The Perceptual World of the Child.* Cambridge, Mass.: Harvard University Press.

Brown, R. 1958. How Shall a Thing be Called? *Psychological Review* 65:14-21.

Cannon, W. B. 1932. *The Wisdom of the Body.* New York: Norton.

Ceccato, S. 1960/1962. Operational Linguistics and Translation. In Ceccato et al. *Linguistic Analysis and Programming for Mechanical Translation.* Milan, Italy: Feltrinelli; and New York: Gordon and Breach.

Craik, K.J.W. 1966. *The Nature of Psychology.* Cambridge, England: The University Press.

Feyerabend, P. 1975. *Against Method.* Atlantic Highlands: Humanities Press.

Flavell, J. H. 1977. *Cognitive Development.* Englewood Cliffs, N.J.: Prentice-Hall.

Gallup, G. G. 1977. Self-Recognition in Primates. *American Psychologist* 32:329-338.

Hanson, N. R. 1958. *Patterns of Discovery.* Cambridge, England: The University Press.

Hebb, D. O. 1975. Science and the World of Imagination. *Canadian Psychological Review* 16:4-11.

Heisenberg, W. 1955. *Das Naturbild der Heutigen Physik.* Hamburg: Rowohlt.

Heisenberg, W. 1971. *Physics and Beyond.* New York: Harper and Row.

Held, R. November 1965. Plasticity in Sensory-Motor Systems. *Scientific American.* Reprinted in *Perception: Mechanisms and Models.* San Francisco: Freeman.

Hilgard, E. R. 1974. Toward a Neo-Dissociation Theory: Multiple Cognitive Controls in Human Functioning. *Perspectives in Biology and Medicine* 17:301-316.

Hume, D. 1963. *An Enquiry Concerning Human Understanding* (1748). New York: Washington Square Press.

James, W. 1955. *Pragmatism* (1907). New York: Meridian Books.

Kuhn, T. S. 1970. *The Structure of Scientific Revolutions.* Chicago: University of Chicago Press.

Maturana, H. R. 1970. Neurophysiology of Cognition. In P. L. Garvin (Ed.). *Cognition: A Multiple View.* New York: Spartan.

McFarland, D. J. 1971. *Feedback Mechanisms in Animal Behavior.* New York: Academic Press.

Mayr, O. 1970. *The Origin of Feedback Control.* Cambridge, Mass.: M.I.T. Press.

Pask, G. 1969. The Meaning of Cybernetics in the Behavioral Sciences. In J. Rose (Ed.). *Progress of Cybernetics.* New York: Gordon and Breach.

Piaget, J. 1971. *La Construction du Réel Chez L'enfant.*

Neuchâtel: Delachaux et Niestlé (1937). English transl. New York: Ballantine.

Piaget, J. 1957. *Six Psychological Studies*. New York: Random House.

Piaget, J. 1972. *The Principles of Genetic Epistemology*. New York: Basic Books.

Powers, W. T. 1973. *Behavior: The Control of Perception*. Chicago: Aldine.

Pritchard, R. M., Heron, W., and Hebb, D. O. 1950. Visual Perception Approached by the Method of Stabilized Images. *Canadian Journal of Psychology* 14:67-77.

Richards, J., and von Glasersfeld, E. 1978. The Control of Perception and the Construction of Reality. *Dialectica*. In press.

Shumaker, N. W. 1977. Conceptual Analysis of Spatial Location as Indicated by Certain English Prepositions. Unpublished dissertation. University of Georgia: Athens.

Trevarthen, C., Hubley, P., and Sheeran, L. 1975. Les Activités Innées du Nourrisson. *La Recherche* 6, no. 56, pp. 447-458.

Varela, F. The Arithmetic of Closure. 1975. *Proceedings of the Third European Meeting on Cybernetics and Systems Research*. Vienna, Austria.

von Foerster, H. 1970. Thoughts and Notes on Cognition. In P. L. Garvin, ed. *Cognition: A Multiple View*. New York: Spartan.

von Foerster, H. 1976. Objects: Tokens for (Eigen) Behaviors. Piaget Jubilee Meeting, Geneva, 1976. Reprinted in *Cybernetics Forum* 8, nos. 3 and 4, pp. 91-96.

von Glasersfeld, E. 1975. Radical Constructivism and Piaget's Concept of Knowledge. *Proceedings of the 1975 Symposium of the Jean Piaget Society*. Philadelphia. In press.

von Glasersfeld, E. 1976. Cybernetics and Cognitive Development. *American Society for Cybernetics Forum* 8, nos. 3 and 4, pp. 115-120.

von Glasersfeld, E. 1977. The Concepts of Adaptation and Viability in a Radical Constructivist Theory of Knowledge. *Seventh Annual Meeting of the Jean Piaget Society*. Philadelphia.

von Uexküll, Jakob. 1933/1970. *Streifzüge durch die Umwelt von Tieren und Menschen.* Frankfurt am Main, Germany: Fischer.

Vurpillot, E. 1972. *Le Monde Visuel du Jeune Enfant.* Paris: Presses Universitaires de France.

Wapner, S. and Werner, H. 1965. An Experimental Approach to Body Perception from the Organismic-Developmental Point of View. In S. Wapner and H. Werner, eds. *The Body Percept.* New York: Random House.

Wiener, N. 1948/1965. *Cybernetics.* Cambridge, Massachusetts: M.I.T. Press.

Zinchenko, V. P., and Vergiles, N. Y. 1972. Formation of Visual Images. *Special Research Report.* New York: Consultants Bureau.

Part 2
Cybernetics and Theories of Assessment

4
Against "Objective" Tests: A Note on the Epistemology Underlying Current Testing Dogma

Hugh G. Petrie

One of the common-sense distinctions in educational testing is between "objective" and "subjective" tests. The former category includes true-false, multiple-choice, mathematical problem solving, matching, and the like, while the latter comprises essay exams, rating scales, interviews, and ordinary observation of students. Clearly all of these tests are used at one time or another and for one purpose or another, and most educators grant that all of them have a place (e.g., Gronlund, 1976, p. 144ff). The important thing is to choose the most appropriate test for measuring the intended student learning. Objective tests tend to be better at measuring knowledge of facts and the possession of certain kinds of definite problem-solving skills, while subjective tests tend to be better for assessing a student's ability to organize, integrate, and express ideas in an effective way. At least, that seems to be the conventional and even textbook wisdom.

And yet, it is tempting to view subjective tests as somehow inferior to objective tests. Subjective tests seem to enjoy a sort of second-class citizenship. They're all right for certain purposes if you can't do any better, but one gets the distinct impression that objective tests are preferred whenever possible. It almost seems that it would be preferable to have a flute student's performance scored by a machine rather than by Rampal; we just haven't been able to build the right machine yet.

Where does this rough-and-ready, yet terribly influential, distinction come from? I suspect the source is primarily from the method of scoring. Anyone, even a machine, can score an objective test, while scoring a subjective test requires human judgment, and somehow, we have come to believe that mindless, mechanical procedures are to be preferred to judgment. How has such a paradoxical situation come about?

One answer is that mechanical evaluation and scoring techniques can give a more dependable basis for making educational judgments than can individual teachers. The individual is believed to be biased and undependable while the machine is unbiased and consistent. And consistency, replicability, and lack of bias must be included in any concept of objectivity. That is why we prefer mechanically scored "objective" tests to judgmentally scored "subjective" tests. A test is "objective" when format, if not content, creates a decidable procedure for determining right and wrong answers.

Subjective and Objective

Two Senses of Objective and Subjective

There are, however, a number of confusions in this way of looking at the distinction between subjective and objective tests. Michael Scriven (1972) has noted one of these. He suggests that the pair "subjective-objective" marks two very different distinctions. On the one hand, the pair refers to the distinction between biased and unbiased. In this sense "objective" is the important term because it indicates the central concept. One is objective when one attempts to keep bias, from whatever source, from creeping into observation, analysis, and argument. It is a term closely associated with logical, rational, intelligent procedures. Being "objective" in this sense means guarding against the intrusion of whims, prejudices, social or class bias, and simple wishful thinking into our knowledge-seeking activities.

When contrasted with "objective" in the sense of unbiased, "subjective" takes on the sense of bias. Of course, one important source of bias is our personal opinions, wants, and desires. We often wish the world were other than it is, and we allow such personal bias to interfere with a rational, objective assessment. We are being "subjective." Notice carefully, however, that although a person's own feelings and internal subjective states may be an important *source* of bias, when used in opposition to "unbiased," "subjective" *means* "biased." It takes its meaning from this opposition and not from the fact that much bias happens to come from personal internal states.

On the other hand, the pair "subjective-objective" can also refer to the distinction between the personal and the interpersonal (or extrapersonal). In this case, "subjective" is the important concept because a trait, or state, or feeling is subjective only if it is a trait, state, or feeling which belongs to a single person. My hunger is a subjective feeling in this sense as is my fondness for chocolate-covered peanuts.

When paired with "subjective" in the sense of personal, "objective" takes on the meaning of *inter*personal. We could, for example, determine how many people like chocolate-covered peanuts as well as determining the specific gravity of water. Notice with this pair that although it may be relatively easy to be objective (unbiased) about interpersonal affairs, when I say that a given feature is objective (interpersonal) I do not automatically rule out the possibility that there may be bias involved in certain determinations of the feature. The average difference between black and white I.Q. scores may be objective (interpersonal), and yet the procedures for determining this may be highly biased. Highly sophisticated statistical techniques have been developed for dealing with the interpersonal, yet unless the interpersonal is also unbiased, the statistical treatment merely quantifies the bias.

Problems arise when these two *different* distinctions get confused. A common confusion is to *automatically* assume that "bias" and "personal" are always present together. Once this mistake is made, it would seem logically impossible to be objective (unbiased) about things that are internal to a given person. And yet a moment's reflection shows this to be patent nonsense. Although we are not always unbiased about our own feelings, sometimes we are, and in many cases the most objective (unbiased) report about some internal state would be our own subjective (personal) introspection of that state. While the feeling of "love" may lead to *other* unreliable conclusions, it would be absurd to suggest that we really need an inter- (or im-) personal machine to tell us when we are *in* love. In short, in some cases the best way to be objective (unbiased) about certain things is to be subjective (personal).

Now I suspect that it is the confusion I have just noted that gives some substance to the feeling that subjective tests are second-class citizens. For subjective tests tend to emphasize personal judgment, and if we are implicitly confusing the personal with the biased, then clearly objective tests are preferred. Recognizing that there are at least two distinctions at work should help immeasurably in removing the temptation to label tests which rely on subjective (personal) judgments as inevitably inferior.

Another confusion also operates, however, and in perhaps an even more interesting way. This is the case in which the "unbiased" is automatically assumed to be present together with the "interpersonal." It is true that *one* way, although clearly not the only way, of avoiding bias is in some instances to rely upon interpersonal rather than personal judgments. The justification of political democracy depends on this fact. Empirical science also relies on the interpersonal to a large extent, but only properly trained scientists are allowed to "vote." Science is, fortunately, not left to majority rule.

Interpersonal Agreement

I believe that this conflation of "unbiased" and "interpersonal" leads to much of the conventional "wisdom" regarding subjective and objective tests in education. I am referring to the pressures to move away from bias by moving toward tests that stress the interpersonal. Machine scoring turns out to be the most inter- (im-?) personal method we have. If we can agree on mechanical scoring procedures, we have effectively eliminated any hint of personal judgment. Furthermore, this "wisdom" is not all foolishness because in many instances a move to the interpersonal *is* a way to reduce bias. But it will not automatically do so, as is suggested when one mistakenly confuses objective (unbiased) with objective (interpersonal).

I want to look more closely at the role of the interpersonal in avoiding bias. Speaking of evaluation techniques that are clearly interpersonal, Gronlund (1976, p. 4) says, "It is not intended that the use of evaluation techniques replace the thoughtful judgments of teachers, but rather that they provide a more dependable basis for making such judgments." One picture which springs to mind upon reading such a passage (and such remarks are commonplace) is that somehow the goal, were it only attainable, would be to find techniques to replace teachers. If only the measurement techniques were available, whenever there was a conflict between teacher and technique, the technique would win.

If that is the picture we are supposed to assume, it is wrong on historical, methodological, and conceptual grounds. It is wrong historically because the development of any evaluative technique, from packaged standardized test to informal classroom quiz, reflects the initial teacher(s) judgment about the appropriateness and validity of the technique. The development of I.Q. tests is a perfect case in point. Items were constructed, selected, and, at least initially revised with reference to the ability of these tests to match paradigm teacher judgments about "bright" and "slow" children. Only after we were quite confident that the evaluation techniques embodied teacher judgments, did we occasionally let the techniques override teacher judgment in borderline cases.

Methodologically, the idea that techniques take precedence over personal judgment is also a mistake. When one tries to develop formal, comprehensive techniques for dealing with, for example, valid arguments in logic, or gravitational attraction in physics, the judgments about paradigm cases of valid arguments and gravitational attraction are prior to the general techniques. These individual cases are what our techniques have to deal with, and if the techniques don't deal with them, we modify the techniques, not our judgments of which are paradigm valid arguments. Only much later in the development of formal, systematic procedures do we occasionally allow the techniques to legislate over an individual judgment in a borderline case. The teacher can accept a few cases where the standardized test ranks students differently from teachers' professional judgments, but imagine the uproar if the test systematically turned teacher judgments upside-down! Would the tests obviously be a more dependable basis for making educational decisions in such a situation than teachers' professional judgments? Not at all!

The picture of technique always overriding judgment is wrong conceptually as well. I have argued elsewhere (Petrie, 1971) that Wittgenstein shows convincingly that agreement in judgments is the logical basis for giving sense to formal, systematic sets of rules or techniques in any area of human activity. Basically, the idea is that agreement in judgments is to be interpreted as similar ways of acting in similar situations and in the end, we train people into these modes of behavior. We do not have any direct access to reality as it is, we can only deal with the representations we construct of it. What prevents wholesale subjectivism is that we must act in the world and our representations must be such as to allow us reasonably effective action or else the representations will be weeded out in an evolutionary way. The important point for my purposes is that, logically, action in the world precedes static, formal representations of the world.

Specifying Educational Outcomes

However, even if one grants the logical priority of active judgment over static, formal technique, the requirement of agreement in judgment upon which evaluative techniques must be based might be seen as pushing one toward more "objective" (interpersonal) modes of testing. Indeed this is one way to read much of the current literature on testing. The emphasis, for example, on the use of educational outcomes as the basis for designing evaluation instruments is a case in point. We are urged to specify the desired outcomes of education, then design our teaching and testing procedures accordingly. We are not supposed simply to think of the "ground to cover" in a course, for that tells us nothing about what difference we believe the covered ground will make to our students. "How should they be changed as a result of our teaching?" is the question to be asked, not, "What processes are they going to undergo?" For the latter question is pointless without at least an implicit answer to the former.

One should specify intended educational outcomes; however, not just any specification will do. Some general instructional outcomes are too general. What are we to make of the goals of becoming a good citizen or knowing biology? The point seems to be that we don't have agreement in judgments about such vague, general goals, and so to be objective in both the interpersonal and lack of bias sense, we need to specify these goals in more detail so we can reach agreement in judgment.

The injunction to define educational outcomes in behavioral terms can then be seen as a way to meet the demand for agreement in judgment. If we cannot always agree when we have educated a good citizen, perhaps we can agree when a student has voted, or has paid taxes and surely those are part of being a good citizen. Or are they? One could conceive of situations where paying taxes, e.g., a poll tax used to discriminate, would *not* be an act of good citizenship.

Similarly, if one could not agree on what being a good biologist is, perhaps one could agree on instances of "classifying such and such as bacteria," and those are part of being a good biologist. Or are they? Would that rule out the recent discovery of a third form of life previously classified as bacteria?

The point here is that there seem to be two forces operating. One force pushes toward more and more specific, more and more atomistic specifications of educational goals in an effort to reach agreement in judgment. However, the other force seems constantly to be reminding us that the "atoms" we thus identify are the kind they are by virtue of fitting into an overall contextual gestalt that cannot be analyzed away into atoms. Only the context gives meaning to the atoms themselves.

This principle is strikingly illustrated by the perceptual ambiguous figure. Consider, for example, the martini-bikini (top of next page). Is the circle, for example, a boy's navel or an olive dropping into a martini glass? We don't decide whether we have a martini by first deciding whether the circle is an olive. On the contrary, the circle becomes an olive in the context of the martini.

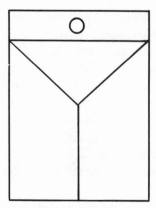

One of the thrusts of behavioral objectives in education thus could be interpreted as an attempt to find context-free atoms upon which we could all agree. If that were possible, then we could specify educational goals in terms of these context-free atoms, plan teaching strategies to lead to these goals, and devise evaluative techniques which would tell us unambiguously when these goals had been reached. How successful has this program been?

I cannot enter here into a detailed polemic against behavioral objectives in education. However, I think it can be fairly stated that the program for finding context-free atoms of behavior related to course content to specify our educational goals and upon which all can agree has not achieved an outstanding success. (See, for example, Smith [1975] for typical critiques.) It is nevertheless instructive to trace the standard moves of the behavioral objectives program.

I have already noted that the first stratagem is to insist that certain common-sense educational goals, such as "training a good biologist," are too vague and general. More specific goals are urged and their specification in behavioral terms is likewise demanded. And to the kinds of objections of context relativity I have raised, the response is to break down the goals into more and more discrete parts. So instead of "identifying bacteria," we might get "identifying such and such a slide as bacteria of a certain kind."

My suspicion is that one can always invent a context, no matter how specific the goals become, that would render the goal inappropriate (Petrie, 1977). I believe it is a general feature of our understanding that specific goals only make sense in presupposed contexts, just as the specific parts of ambiguous figures only make sense given one or the other of the gestalts. If this is so, then the behavioral program of basing agreement on judgments in atomistic elements of teaching and learning is misguided. We will have to presuppose the agreement in judgment on the larger gestalt to even give sense to what the bits and pieces are. However, to pursue that here would take me too far afield. Instead, I shall try to untangle some of the educational presuppositions and implications which seem to accompany the behavioral objectives bandwagon.

Problems with Educational Outcomes

In the first place, the effort to gain agreement in judgment seems to lead not only to smaller and smaller units of analysis, but also to more and more standardized cases. People are more apt to agree on the tried and true than on the novel and creative. And despite some lip service paid to using learning in new situations (transfer of training), the innovative response is clearly discriminated against when one goes the behavioral objectives route.

This tendency to exclude innovative, yet appropriate, responses from the category of "right answer" is heightened by the injunction to tie one's testing procedures closely to specific and behaviorally stated goals. Gronlund (1976, p. 60) says, "The final step in the evaluation process is to *select or develop evaluation instruments that provide the most direct evidence concerning the attainment of each specific learning outcome.*" Later in that chapter he indicates that, for example, if the learning outcome says the student is to "supply" a definition, then the test must ask the student to *supply*, rather than, e.g., *select* a definition.

The advantage of this close link between learning outcome and testing procedure is supposed to lie in the clarity and precision thus afforded the teaching, learning, and evaluating processes. The teacher will know exactly what to teach, the student will know what to learn, and the evaluator will know how to test. The disadvantage, however, comes from the more and more atomistic approach taken in specifying learning outcomes. In an effort to secure the requisite agreement in judgment, the content of the subject and the behaviors associated with learning the subject are analyzed into smaller and smaller and more and more standard learning outcomes. Since the evaluation techniques are tied precisely to the learning outcomes, the test, too, will emphasize the fragmented and the standard as opposed to the integrated and the innovative. Every effort to avoid such a routinization will be a potential threat to the agreement in judgment which must underlie the objective (unbiased) nature of the test. It is a no-win situation.

Another way of making the same point is to note the extreme temptations to "teach to the test" in such a situation. The more fervently one believes that the specific intended learning outcomes should be logically tied to the test, the less outrageous will teaching to the test seem. After all, those specific test behaviors are the goals of the course. Indeed, Stake (1973, p. 207) has noted that the performance contractor in the Texarkana project defended himself against charges of teaching for the test by noting that "teaching and testing had been directed toward the same specific goals, as should be the case in a good performance contract." Teaching to the test becomes virtually a logical injunction!

There is a second educational effect of conventional testing wisdom. The implicit model of testing for learning seems to be a sampling from a field of predetermined possible responses. The total field is presumably determined in principle by the subject matter; one supposes that the student has acquired some, if not all, of these responses, and the tester attempts to sample the student's response repertoire to see how closely it matches the total field. This picture of the situation gives rise to a whole host of puzzles regarding determination of "the" field of study, what constitutes a representative sample, how to sample a student's repertoire, and so on.

The major difficulty, however, seems to me to lie in the implications concerning how what has been learned gets applied to new situations—the so-called transfer of training question. How does a student recognize a new situation as one in which old principles are appropriate? Gronlund, for example (1976, p. 33), admits that an infinite number of possible learning outcomes can be specified for each general objective. This is, presumably, because new situations can vary indefinitely. There are logical questions of how to specify an infinite set without making use of precisely those general goals one is trying to specify, but let me waive *that* objection.

Somehow, the student must recognize the test question as sufficiently like what has been learned to call forth a response. Next the student must carefully analyze the new, transfer situation determining in what respects it is like, and in what respects unlike, what has gone before. Then the appropriate response from the infinitude available must be chosen and applied to the new situation. Of course, we are typically wholly unaware of such delicate analysis of situation, choice of response, and application to new context. All of that would have to occur unconsciously. The fact to be explained is that we can and do use what we have learned in an indefinite number of new situations. We are incredibly adaptable. The question is whether the picture of selecting from an infinity of preexisting responses the one which just matches the given situation adequately accounts for the fact of transfer. Surely, we might at least consider alternatives.

Finally, the conventional wisdom on tests leads one to a picture of the repertoire of learnings being sampled as consisting of stable, static elements—facts, concepts, methodologies, skills, understandings, and so on. Gronlund again (1976, p. 29) distinguishes sharply between the process of learning—the educational experiences undergone—and the products of learning—the knowledge and skills achieved. It is the products which must be utilized in framing learning outcomes. It is the products for which we must test. It makes little difference if we have covered certain material if nothing has happened to change our students. So in evaluation we must look to see what changes have occurred and not simply list the educational processes carried out.

Now there is nothing really wrong with such advice. The old educational saw that there can be no real teaching without learning reminds us that the object of our instructional and learning processes must in the end be changes in the students. Too much education has gone on with a simple reference to what the teacher has done—never mind what the pupil has accomplished.

However, the pernicious outcome of this emphasis on outcomes is that we may be tempted to view the products of learning as static, relatively stable atoms, in short, as "things" —knowledge, skills, understandings, and the like. However, such a view is not a logically necessary result of recognizing the process-product distinction in learning. The product of learning may well be that students now have new ways of processing their experience. The product of a process may be another process. Perhaps we should speak not of knowledge, but of the processes of knowing (see Campbell, 1959, 1974), not of skills, but of activities, not of understandings, but of the process of understanding.

I am not urging that we concentrate on the *process* of learning itself, but rather, that we consider the possibility that the *product* of learning may well be processes, rather than substances. As Stephen Toulmin says in the epigram to his provocative book, *Human Understanding* (Toulmin, 1972, p. x) "A man demonstrates his rationality not by a commitment to fixed ideas, stereotyped procedures, or immutable concepts, but by the manner in which, and the occasions on which, he changes those ideas, procedures, and concepts."

There are two reasons which to me have emerged from the discussion thus far that counsel toward considering knowledge processes rather than knowledge products as basic to the evaluative situation. First, the agreements in judgment which seem to underlie our ability to be objective in any field of human activity require physical and mental *action* in the world and not mere copying of the world. In a sense, we must contribute to the construction of our knowledge. This theme is common from the philosopher, Kant, through the psychologist, Piaget, to the devotees of open education. Second, this construction seems to take place not through the application of set procedures, but through the activities of seeing things as belonging to certain contexts. One and the same "thing" (the circle) can be seen as olive or navel depending on the context of activities in which we might place it. One and the same thing (a story in an elementary reader) can be seen as exemplifying family values or as sexist depending on the context in which we read the story.

The Cybernetic Alternative

I contend that a cybernetic approach to testing for learning gives promise of overcoming the problems I have uncovered with the conventional view of what testing for learning is all about. The cybernetic view does, I believe, take knowledge as basically a process rather than a substance. In a straightforward way a cybernetic view shows how our knowledge is constructed through our activities and how feedback loops provide the context for interpreting specific examples of action. More to the point for education, cybernetics shows how the novel and innovative response in an evaluative setting can be just as objective as the standard and paradigmatic. The phenomenon of transfer of training becomes transparent in a cybernetic setting, for within its effective range of control, what feedback loops do is control for the kinds of variations found in typical transfer tasks. Finally, the puzzles of how the evaluator samples from an infinite repertoire disappear. On the cybernetic view, one does not have a set of atomistic responses from which to choose, but rather a control system whose operation is designed to counteract disturbances.

What I will do in the remainder of this chapter is sketch the basic model of the testing process from a cybernetic perspective. I will try to show how the difficulties I raised above for the conventional view can be accommodated within the cybernetic model and how the subjective-objective distinction among types of tests with which I began this paper collapses when viewed from the cybernetic perspective.

I shall not spend the time outlining the cybernetic perspective itself but shall assume the model described with great clarity by William Powers in his *Behavior: The Control of Perception* (Powers, 1973) and summarized by him in this volume. My thesis is simple. The cybernetic or control system approach gives promise of overcoming the accumulated conceptual and empirical difficulties of the conventional approaches to testing for learning and at the same time points to fruitful new directions for expanding our conceptions of what objective (unbiased) testing must be like. Finally the cybernetic approach accepts in the main the current common-sense forms of testing and merely reinterprets what we are doing when we engage in standard testing practice. No new model such as the one I am proposing can ignore what has proven successful and fruitful under past paradigms. What it can do is to point to new directions to proceed from here. With that methodological preamble, let me begin.

I have described the conventionally accepted model of testing for learning as sampling from an hypothesized infinite repertoire of learned atomistic responses. The cybernetic model of testing for learning can perhaps best be described as introducing a disturbance to an hypothesized knowledge process and observing to see if the disturbance is counteracted, just as a thermostat counteracts the disturbance of falling temperature by turning on the furnace. Basically, I am suggesting that for each of the typical sorts of things we learn and come to know, a control system (or system of control systems) can be hypothesized constituting that knowledge. Coming to know is coming to have the appropriate control system. Knowing is operating with the control system or, in the dispositional mode, is being ready to operate with the control system if a disturbance occurs.

I want to stress that what a control system *does*, as Powers so beautifully illustrates in the title of his book, is to control perceptions by behavior. Control systems do *not* delicately vary their outputs to match the details of varying situations. Rather, when they sense a disturbance in the quantity they control, they drive their outputs relatively blindly. If the system is at all well adapted to typical ecologies in which it finds itself, the outputs will operate through the environment to counteract the disturbance. The control system wants to "perceive" a certain state and will operate to the limit of its capacity in attempting to perceive that state. Even the lowly thermostat exemplifies this crucial feature. *What* the thermostat does is to control the ambient temperature, and it operates the furnace in case the sensed temperature differs enough from the set temperature. And it will do so whether or not the house is well, or poorly, insulated, whether or not there is an open window or a lamp near the thermostat, and whether or not there is a burner clogged on the furnace. The system will simply drive its output if it senses a difference (or disturbance) between what is actually perceived and what the system wants to perceive. Even though a *causal* analysis of the system may go from input through the comparison of input with reference signal to the output and thence through the system's environment back to the input, the *explanatory* direction is just the opposite. The line of control runs through the perceptual side of the system (Powers, 1973; Petrie, 1974; Ryan, 1970). *What* the system does is control its inputs or perceptions.

How might this work in the case of testing for learning? Consider first the knowledge of facts. On the cybernetic model, knowing a fact is being in possession of a feedback system which represents that fact as a reference signal in the system. The input function of the cybernetic system monitors the environment for the degree to which it is like the given fact, and if that perception does not match the reference signal, an output will occur that can change the environment to bring perception and reference signal into line. For example, if someone knows that plants need sunshine to grow and perceives a plant in the dark, he'll move it, conclude the plant won't grow, or do something else which removes the disturbance.

How does one test for knowledge of facts? The technique is to devise some perceptual situation such that if the student being tested knows the fact, the situation will be perceived as containing a disturbance to the hypothesized cybernetic knowledge process that represents the fact. All the evaluator has to do is observe whether the student's output tends to counteract the disturbance or not. If it does, then the fact is probably known; if not, the student probably doesn't know the fact. The approach is not fool-proof. The disturbance may be removed fortuitously (e.g., the student may guess when the fact is not known), or the student may fail to remove the disturbance even though the fact is known (e.g., the test question may be misunderstood). But this is no more a limitation on the cybernetic than it is on the conventional approach.

Of course, most test situations are constructed to guarantee the motivation of the student and the likelihood that the control system representing the fact will be engaged if the student knows the fact. Thus, the disturbance might be a true-false test with the item being "The Declaration of Independence was signed in 1776." In this case, marking "false" would constitute a disturbance and if the student knows the fact, the disturbance will be avoided rather than directly counteracted.

What is the situation with regard to the learning of concepts? Once again the model suggests that a concept is represented by a cybernetic control system. Suppose the task is to learn the concept of "goose" where geese have to be distinguished from ducks and swans (see Kuhn, 1974). In this case, if one has learned the concept of "goose" then perceptual examples of geese will be recognized as such. A swan would constitute a disturbance to the "goose" control system possibly because of the swan's arching neck. The disturbance would be removed by classifying it as "non-goose." A duck might disturb the goose control system because of its shorter neck. Again the disturbance could be removed by excluding the instance from the concept.

How does one test for knowledge of concepts? He can introduce disturbances and see if they are counteracted or give samples of positive and negative instances of geese and see whether the disturbances are corrected or avoided. A multiple choice question could also be used, as,

A goose is a
   a) bird
   b) fish
   c) mammal
   d) none of the above.

Notice the close connection between concepts and propositions on the control system model. Recognizing certain perceptual experiences as instances of concepts seems to involve making judgments of the sort, "This is a goose." At the same time instances of concepts stand in many relations to other items in the environment. So concepts figure in many propositions, many of which would, if false, constitute disturbances to controlling for the concept itself. Thus if an object were not even a bird, it could not be a goose.

On the other hand, it used to be thought that whiteness was always associated with swans. The black swans of Australia did not constitute a large enough disturbance, however, to render those birds non-swans. In this way a rough and ready categorization of essential and accidental properties of any concept can be worked out. Notice, however, that the categorization will be relative to an individual's system of control systems. Does the absence of a given property cause a large enough disturbance to remove the example from the effective range of control of the hypothesized control system (e.g., this object is not a bird)? If so, the property is essential. If the property's absence leads rather to corrective behavior (e.g., the acceptance of black swans), then the property is accidental *for the given system* of control systems.

How does understanding fit into the control system model? Items of varying complexity can be understood—concepts, facts, people, theories, etc. Each of these needs to be analyzed to determine just what is at stake. Nevertheless, some general comments are probably possible. Understanding generally involves placing something in a larger context (Halstead, 1975). In control system terms, this means that when someone understands something, there is a control system nested within a larger complex (probably hierarchical) of control systems. Thus if one not only knows that plants need sunshine to grow, but also understands why, it means that some knowledge of the theory of photosynthesis is also part of the student's control systems and further that these control systems subsume the lower-order facts of growth in sunshine.

How does one test for understanding on the cybernetic model? Because of the way larger contexts provide ways of assimilating whole classes of experience, testing for understanding is less susceptible to "objective" tests than testing for factual knowledge. Disturbances to understanding can occur in a large number of connected ways, as can the corrections to those disturbances. One could demonstrate an understanding of photosynthesis by articulating the theory, by designing appropriate "growth" lights to take the place of sunshine, by conducting appropriate experiments on photosynthesis, and so on and on.

On the conventional view of testing for learning, testing for understanding tends to move one into the area of "subjective" tests. But this can now be seen as a highly misleading way of putting the point. On the cybernetic view, the test is always to introduce a disturbance and see if it is corrected. Thus tests for understanding are just as objective (unbiased) as are tests for knowledge of facts. The difference is that the available area for introducing disturbances to control systems representing understanding is so much larger and so many more things will count as corrections to the disturbance.

Consider the analogy with the thermostat. It controls temperature alone. Suppose we add a humidistat to control humidity and tie both the thermostat and humidistat together with a "comfortstat" that controls a complicated combination of temperature and humidity, so that a whole range of varying combinations of temperature and humidity could satisfy the comfortstat. The comfortstat represents an analogue of "understanding" temperature and humidity relations. The ways of disturbing this system are vastly increased over the ways of disturbing the thermostat alone (analogous to a single fact). Similarly, the ways of correcting disturbances are much greater. We can change temperature, or humidity, or various combinations of them. Imagine what would happen as we increased the interrelatedness (understanding potential) of such a system. Clearly the attempt to specify in advance the variety of specific potential disturbances and corrections becomes impossible. Rather, the global feature of "comfort" becomes the explanatory concept.

Another item sometimes said to be taught, learned, and tested for is methodology. This, too, covers the waterfront just as does "understanding." Different fields have different methodologies, and there are a host of degrees of explicitness of methodology from formal algorithms to less precise heuristics to "the scientific method" which may itself change over time. Once more the cybernetic view treats methodologies as represented by control systems (or systems of control systems). The methodology for adding a column of figures is fairly precise and the activities performed in that process are easily checked, both at the time of performance and subsequently. At the more general level of "good science," where physicists are, for example, debating the fruitfulness of searching for ever more fundamental particles, "disturbances" and "corrections" will be much more idiosyncratically determined.

How does one test for a given methodology on the cybernetic view? Once again, see how disturbances are corrected. With something as explicit as the rules for addition, the task is easy. Give problems and see how the student avoids disturbances. Be sure to throw in some "hard" ones, too, in which the disturbances are difficult to catch. For less precise methods, such as heuristics, again introduce disturbances and see how they are corrected. Various chess moves and situations can be seen as disturbances to the heuristics of how to play good chess. So far, chess masters seem to grasp the heuristics of chess much better than do chess-playing computer programs. Is it because chess programs must analyze the heuristics into digital processes, whereas human heuristics work on an analogical gestaltist basis? I tend to think so. At the level of "good physics," only history ultimately can judge whether a proposed "correction" really is one. Did it, in the end, work out?

A particularly interesting class of items taught and learned is commonly called skills. Consider the ability to drive a car, for example. What does such an ability look like on the cybernetic model? Take the simple aspect of steering. Most drivers, if they think about it, will say that they steer by maintaining a certain perceptual relationship, e.g., keeping the hood ornament on the right hand edge of the lane in which one is driving. Indeed grasping such a relationship is a great advance in learning to drive. One no longer has to analyze the situation and decide what to do next at each moment in the driving sequence. Indeed, when one does analyze and "think about" one's driving by "applying" the principles, overreaction almost invariably ensues. The good driver does not say, "Aha, a curve to the right of about 30 degrees, so, given the steering ratio of my car, I must turn the steering wheel to the right about 10 degrees." Rather the driver notices a disturbance to the desired perceptual pattern and acts until the ornament gets back on the edge of the lane. The driver controls perceptions, not outputs.

Notice, too, how much easier the cybernetic view makes the account of handling situations which are never analyzed except insofar as they disturb the desired perceptual relation of ornament to edge of road. Consider a crosswind. The driver need never (and often does not) recognize there is a crosswind. But insofar as the wind affects the position of the ornament relative to the edge of the road, the driver will automatically correct the disturbance. Similar remarks apply to road conditions, looseness in the steering mechanism, and so on. The driver controls perceptions, not outputs.

How do we test for such skills? In the driving case, it's easy. There are enough natural disturbances in driving so that we put an examiner in the seat beside the driver and let him observe how the driver counteracts the disturbances.

One can also easily see the difference between skills which may be possessed and tendencies or habits which we hope will be exercised. The *ability* to keep household accounts may be checked by classroom tests; the *tendency* to do so would require what might be considered an unwarranted invasion of privacy. On the cybernetic view, the difference can be seen as a difference in *what* is being disturbed, the control system which wants to get a good grade in a school subject or the control system for keeping track of day-to-day expenses (Petrie, 1974).

In either case, the cybernetic model of testing for performance skills seems *prima facie* much more realistic than the conventional model. We do not learn the principles of skills and then apply them. Rather we acquire certain perceptual quantities to control and correct for disturbances. One could not possibly specify all the behaviors that go into correctly steering a car and then go about testing for each of them. Rather we know perfectly well what steering a car properly means, and can see when someone does it even if the disturbance is a blowout or a child darting into the street after a loose ball.

A More Complicated Example

None of the examples of tests one might use on the cybernetic model has differed much, if at all, from the kinds of tests one might use on the conventional model. I have suggested multiple-choice, true-false, identification, skill demonstration, and the like; standard testing uses these types too, and it might be objected that all I have done is to introduce a jargon-loaded way of talking about these familiar kinds of tests.

I have already admitted that any new theoretical model must handle the standard examples in the field. Any proposed new theory that said in effect that everything we've been doing has been wrong would, for that reason, be highly suspect, so the cybernetic view must accept most standard testing procedures. It is in the borderline cases and in giving us hints on how to extend our understanding that theories will differ. In this section I want to try to sketch a borderline case where conceptualizing the testing situation under the conventional versus the cybernetic models might lead to different results.

Consider the learning of fractions. This task is typically a difficult one for many students. One of the more difficult aspects is getting the student to grasp the idea that a whole can be cut up into parts (fractions) and that these fractions make up the whole. A typical test item at the beginning stages of teaching fractions might go as follows: Sue, Bill, and Mary went to a pizza parlor to order a large pizza. If they divided it equally, how much did each one receive? The answer is, of course, one-third. This kind of test item is probably repeated in slightly different formats dozens of times during a student's learning fractions. One varies the food and the number of people, but the test item remains basically the same.

And yet, as teachers well know, students can become fairly proficient on this type of item and yet not fully grasp the idea that those three thirds make up the whole pizza. On the conventional model, one simply searches for other preexisting responses to situations which call for different and perhaps more complicated applications of the rule of dividing the food by the number of people. One perhaps also hopes that the division of food will generalize to the division of toys, money, jobs, or whatever. But the basic concept is that the rule is applied in new situations.

What might a test item look like on the cybernetic model of introducing a disturbance to an hypothesized control system? Suppose the concept being tested for is the part-whole relationship. Consider the following item: Sue, Bill, and Mary went to a pizza parlor and ordered a large pizza. Sue said, "I want one-third of the pizza"; Bill said, "I want one-third of the pizza"; and, Mary said, "I want two-thirds of the pizza." Can each child receive what he or she wants?

In this item a disturbance to the whole-part relationship has been introduced and how the child corrects the disturbance will show whether or not the concept has been learned. The item can be varied in a number of ways and leads itself easily to follow-up questions. For example, one might add, "If so, will there be any left? How much?" "If not, why not?"

The item can then be varied by having each of the children ask for one-fourth of the pizza. Then with the follow-up questions, a set of parts which do not add up to the whole can be identified. This is another, different, disturbance to the part-whole concept for which we are testing. The point is not that the cybernetic view generates tests or test items which could not in principle be generated under the conventional model, but rather that it sets us off in a slightly different, and, I think, more fruitful direction.

The reaction to this kind of item by the advocates of the conventional model of testing will be that they too could have come up with the item. It requires just a complicated bit of transfer of training. It requires the student to select from a broader response repertoire. And yet such a reply doesn't quite ring true. Intuitively one is inclined to say that the student hasn't really understood the part-whole relationship until he or she can answer such test items. It's not that the test requires a new application; it's rather that the test gets at the concept directly.

If this sort of example is at all persuasive, I suggest it is because it makes direct use of the model of removing a disturbance rather than the model of selecting from a repertoire of responses. However, I realize no single example can possibly make my case. Rather it is the general theory or model with which one approaches each case that makes the difference. For that reason, I want to consider in the next section how the cybernetic model deals with the general problems associated with the conventional model.

Cybernetics and Innovation,
Transfer of Training, and Knowledge Processes

Recall the three main difficulties I uncovered with the conventional model of testing for learning. These were, first, that the conventional model finds it tremendously difficult to find room for appropriate, yet innovative, test responses. The push for standardization and stereotyping of response is strong. Second, the conventional view with its pictures of sampling from a predetermined repertoire of atomistic responses renders transfer of training quite problematic. The idea that somehow we (unconsciously) analyze each new situation and then select just the right response from the repertoire seems dubious at best and simply a redescription of the problem at worst. Third, the conventional view pictures a relatively stable product as the result of the learning process, and it is that product that is sampled during testing. I have urged that there is strong reason for considering knowledge itself to be a process rather than a structure. Thus if we are testing for knowledge, we are testing for certain kinds of processes.

How does the cybernetic model of testing for learning fare

with these difficulties? The picture of introducing a disturbance to a hypothesized control system and checking to see
if it is counteracted or avoided handles the novel response
problem in a most illuminating way. Not only does the cybernetic model wait to see what the response is before deciding
whether it's appropriate, it also gives a method for determining whether the response is appropriate. Does it tend to
remove the disturbance? Thus, the model does have empirical
consequences and the existence of hypothesized control systems can be tested. The very mark of human rationality
seems to be its adaptability to an indefinite variety of circumstances. In short, the *novel* answer to "test" situations is the
core of our concept of knowledge. Instead of its being an
unwelcome intruder for whom we must somehow find room
in the conventional model of testing, the novel answer is the
master of the house on the cybernetic view. By giving pride
of place conceptually to this central feature of human adaptability, the cybernetic model is in a very clear sense a more
human approach to testing for learning than the conventional
approach. How could we ever have thought that we could
select from among an infinity of potential responses anyway?
Computers may check off lists; humans seldom do.

The case with transfer of training is very similar. Transfer
of training is a problem on the conventional view but becomes a paradigmatic feature of the cybernetic view. On the
conventional view it is hard to see how one recognizes the
new situation as sufficiently like the paradigm situation in
which the knowledge was acquired to call forth an appropri-
ately adjusted response. One must "apply" knowledge to new
situations and the temptation is great to assume that another
piece of knowledge is present that tells us when and how to
apply our original knowledge. But in this way lies a dark and
infinite regress. For we need also to know when and how to
apply the rules of application, and off we go.

But the regress generated by viewing the transfer problem
as one in which we must "apply" knowledge simply disappears on the cybernetic view. For on the cybernetic view there
is not the slightest temptation to speak of applying knowledge
in new situations. On the contrary, the situation is perceived

as more or less like the paradigmatic learned situation, and if the control system is operating, the student will simply behave in ways that reduce the "distance" between the perceived and the desired situation. The thermostat causes the furnace to go on, which reduces the difference between the perceived ambient temperature and the thermostat setting. The car wheel is turned to reduce the perceived distance between the hood ornament and the edge of the road. The physics student learns to see the problems at the end of the chapter in terms of the principles learned in the chapter (Petrie, 1976; Kuhn 1974). In short, a cybernetic system operates to change the environment to bring it closer to the organizing principle or reference signal of the system. One does not "apply" knowledge at all, and so there is no problem of how application can occur in new situations.

Finally, the fact that a control system is operative in the production of the quantities it controls clearly indicates that one is dealing with a knowledge process and not with a static structure of knowledge. Control systems exhibit on their face the contribution of the system to the construction of knowledge. Notice that it is only a *contribution* to knowledge and not the whole constitution of it. If a thermostat is hooked up to an inefficient furnace in a poorly insulated house during very cold weather, it may be unable to stablize the ambient temperature at 68° F, although it may tend in that direction. Similarly we cannot all, simply by wishing it so, run a four-minute mile or win a Nobel prize in physics. Cybernetics shows how control systems perceive in the environment whatever it is they are controlling for and how they can change the environment *within limits* to become more like what is being controlled for. The limits are set by the world as it is, natural and social.

Objective and Subjective Tests Reconsidered

To conclude, I shall return to the distinction between objective and subjective tests with which I began this paper. In a very real sense the distinction between mechanical and judgmental scoring procedures no longer seems very important. Indeed, all evaluative measures depend at base upon agreement in judgment, and so, if anything, "subjective" tests are more central to evaluation than "objective" tests. But the question then arose as to what the agreement in judgments was agreement about—a static repertoire of atomistic responses, or the correction or avoidance of disturbances to control systems. I have urged that the cybernetic approach gives promise of avoiding some of the problems with the conventional approach.

No new theory of testing would have much plausibility if it urged a wholesale rejection of the kinds of testing currently in use. It is highly unlikely that our best professional practice, accumulated over the years by a trial and error process, is largely wrong. It wouldn't have survived were that the case. Nevertheless, when it comes to understanding our common practice and extending it in new directions, different theories do make a difference. On a global scale this is reflected by the kind of second-class citizenship enjoyed by "subjective" tests under the conventional theory of testing. On the conventional view we must justify using "subjective" tests because of our inability to find "objective" ones. On the cybernetic view the burden of proof is reversed. The basic testing situation is seeing if disturbances are corrected *in whatever way the student sees fit*. The novel response rather than the typical one is the standard condition. On the cybernetic view we must justify using objective tests that limit the testing situation so that only a few responses will count as "right." No doubt such a justification can be given in certain cases, but on the cybernetic view, it *must* be given.

Gronlund (1976, p. 149) has interesting comments on the effect "objective and subjective" tests have on the control of student responses. He admits that an objective test "limits pupil to type of response called for." However, he seems to view this as a virtue because he continues that this "prevents bluffing and avoids influence of writing skill." His comments on the essay test concerning its control of pupil response are that "freedom to respond in own words enables bluffing and writing skill to influence the score." Clearly, the cybernetic approach would render almost the opposite judgment on the value of structuring the pupil's responses. If *what* is being done in testing is seeing if and how disturbances are counteracted, then limiting the ways of counteracting the disturbances is *prima facie* wrong and can be justified only in special circumstances.

Multiple-choice tests, for example, will continue to be used about as much as they are now. But in the cybernetic view they are seen for what they are, an often artificial limiting so that only five responses seem appropriate for removing disturbances. It helps, of course, to tell the student to choose the "best" response, but the point is that the ways of removing disturbances have been set by the tester. As is granted even under the conventional view, multiple-choice tests are best in content areas where the facts are pretty well agreed. When used to test for more complex learning such as understanding or reasoning called for is fairly unitary and stereotypical. If understanding in an area is complex and unpredictable, the use of multiple-choice exams will distort the subject matter. Thus, using multiple-choice exams in mathematical reasoning is probably all right, but their use in testing for the interpretation of a poem would be misleading since the interpretations have been limited.

The true-false test is even more constricting than the multiple-choice exam. It presupposes a clear binary decision about a given item. Again this may be true for some limited fields and for certain limited areas of those fields, but the true-false exam begins to mislead when it is extended beyond obviously binary decisions. I shouldn't be surprised if the barbarisms "more true," "less false," and the like are not somehow linked to trying to extend true-false items beyond their appropriate range.

Matching tests are useful for checking fine discriminations. If a host of similar items in one list "go with" certain items in another list, making sure these lists are matched is a useful way of checking our facts. A typical example is to match explorers with countries in a social studies test. Once again, the cybernetic view can account for successful performance in an absolutely straightforward way. Putting the country with the proper explorer literally removes the disturbance caused by having the column of explorers not match the column of countries. However, once more the subject areas in which such tests can be justified are probably a good deal fewer than are commonly believed. And the burden of proof is on those who would expand matching tests beyond a limited arena.

Completion or short answer essay tests are an interesting category. Viewed conventionally, they are probably closer to "objective" tests in that a fairly definite answer is usually sought by the examiner. Nevertheless, the student can respond as he or she sees fit. A wrong answer on the conventional view is just a wrong choice of response. On the cybernetic view, however, the student believes that the answer given will remove the disturbance caused by the blank in the completion exercise. This almost forces the teacher to ask, "What control system *was* operating for the student?" Valuable clues are available for diagnosing the student's mistake. What would the student have to believe for the wrong answer to appear right? Of course, good teachers have always used wrong answers diagnostically. It's just that the theory of selecting from a repertoire of responses gives us no guidance as to how to diagnose the error. The cybernetic view, on the other hand, asks the evaluator to view the response as attempted correction: in virtue of what control system would it be a correction?

One also needs to consider the test response *both* from the point of view of what the student believes is being controlled and from the point of view of the collective understanding the teacher is testing for. In short, there are two cybernetic systems in operation—the student's and the teacher's. Do they control the same quantity? Essay tests bring out this duality very nicely. Because of the relative lack of prespecified structure in an essay exam, the student can remove the disturbance in whatever way seems most appropriate to the student.

The teacher-evaluator probably has a *better* view of what control system the student possesses from an essay test than from a multiple choice or completion exam. In the essay test the student demonstrates in a fairly complex way how his or her cybernetic control systems are organized. Literally, more of the "person" can be discerned through an essay test than through "objective" tests. Concomitantly, the teacher-evaluator can judge the extent to which the student's control systems match up with the teacher's (assuming the teacher embodies the collective disciplinary wisdom being taught). In this way the phenomenon of teachers learning something from their students on essay tests is explained by the fact that the teacher must decide whether the student's effort causes any disturbance in the teacher's control systems.

Can the student "bluff" more easily on an essay test? In a sense, he obviously can. But the bluffing will only be effective on less than competent teachers whose *own* control systems do not enable them to distinguish the glib from the insightful. "Objective" tests with their mechanical scoring procedures do tend to protect student assessment from relatively incompetent teachers, but at the cost of limiting the more competent students. It's not clear that such a trade-off is always in the best interests of education.

Intuitively, university professors recognize the value of the oral exam as used, for example, in the defense of a doctoral dissertation. The oral exam, far from going off on tangents and not "covering the ground," enables the evaluators to explore in some detail the student's cognitive functioning. The professor asks a question introducing a disturbance into the student's control systems. The student responds in a way he believes will remove the disturbance. But does it from the evaluator's point of view? Well, if the student really has "got it," and responds in the way he or she did, then this further question should elicit such and such a correcting response. And the process can be iterated again and again. The depth and complexity of modes of correcting disturbances that can be explored in an oral exam is truly amazing. Surface answers will not do. One can "cram" for an "objective" test, one cannot "cram" for an oral. The former gets at breadth, but probably in a superficial way. The latter gets at the enduring knowledge processes of the student.

The much maligned interview also turns out to be a very potent testing device on the cybernetic view. Its advantages are very similar to those of the oral doctoral exam. The ways in which disturbances are corrected by the interviewee tell a great deal about the knowledge processes likely to be employed later on. How does the candidate react to a change of pace? Does the person give short or long answers? What specific kinds of things does the interviewee know? If one were sampling from a repertoire of atomistic responses, the interview would probably be incredibly inefficient and subjective. But if one is looking to see if and how disturbances to control systems are corrected, the interview can pursue these in great depth.

One can even test by observation, particularly by participant-observation. I suspect that most day-to-day evaluations by classroom teachers are of this type. Classroom teachers, especially in the elementary grades, interact with their students in a wide variety of contexts. They really can get to know their students, and they are constantly introducing disturbances, observing how these are corrected, and devising remedial work. The difference between observer and participant-observer on the cybernetic view is the difference between having to wait to see how natural disturbances are corrected and being able to introduce those disturbances. The classroom teacher is probably a paradigm case of the participant-observer category of evaluator.

One of the traditional objections to the observer, or even participant-observer, methodologies is that the observations tend to be subjective, i.e., couched in the observer's categories. This objection is easily met on the cybernetic view. Any hypothesis about what the student knows will be cast in the observer's categories. However, there is a check for the adequacy of that characterization. Introduce what would be a disturbance if the hypothesized control system is operative in the student and see if it is counteracted. Of course, mistakes are still possible. An hypothesized system may be close enough to the actual system to be judged as present on the basis of the disturbances introduced when it actually is not. But this possibility of error always obtains in empirical sciences. It is sometimes very difficult, although not in principle impossible, to disentangle competing hypotheses. The cybernetic view does indicate the general principles to be followed in disentangling the hypotheses.

Another objection to observational methods has been that sometimes what people really know and believe is not what they say. So even if one asks a student how *he* views the situation, that may not reflect his "real" cognitive state. The cybernetic approach seems to me to obviate that criticism by treating the correction of disturbances in a much broader context than simply what people say. The cybernetic approach concentrates on what people do. What people say is part of what they do, but only part. The general formula of introducing a disturbance and seeing how it is counteracted draws attention to the whole field of action, not just verbal actions.

The use of rating scales and check lists in an effort to make the observation more "objective" will probably only end up in blinding the observer to other important features that do seem to be making a difference. Of course, the other side of that coin is that checklists can perhaps help the inexperienced observer keep track of the important things to be watched for.

The "case-study" evaluation utilizing observational techniques in a central role is a perfectly valid mode of evaluation. When competently undertaken, it will reflect what the actors know and do. In brief, it will illuminate what is going on in the sense that this is what the actors are actually doing. For on the cybernetic view the evaluation introduces a disturbance to an hypothesized control system and sees if it is corrected. Case studies can be generalized precisely to the extent that similar people in similar situations tend to *do* the same things. Notice carefully that what someone *does* is defined not in terms of behavioral effects—those could well vary from situation to situation—but rather in terms of the quantities the actor is controlling. Thus, providing remedial classes in one context, e.g., a community college, may be just as much the teaching of good writing as refusing to provide such classes in a different context, e.g., a selective private college. The level of analysis of what is going on must always be in terms on what disturbances will be corrected.

In summary, the cybernetic model of testing for learning

promises a number of advantages over the conventional model. The conventional picture of sampling from an infinite set of discrete responses seems to generate problems of how to evaluate innovative responses and how to understand transfers of training. It also presupposes the somewhat dubious idea of static knowledge structures. The cybernetic view of observing to see if and how disturbances are removed seems to solve all of these problems at a stroke. The common wisdom of dividing tests into subjective and objective is misguided. All evaluation depends on agreement in judgments among those who know what the activity being evaluated is. "Subjective" tests turn out to be closer to what students actually know and can do and are, and therefore are more human (not merely more humane) in an absolutely straightforward sense.

In changing from the conventional to the cybernetic view, the burden of proof is shifted radically. No longer must one justify essay tests because really objective tests are not available. On the contrary, one must justify using objective tests by trying to show that the stereotypical responses encouraged are really all right in the context. Finally, I am not claiming that one must do away with the commonly accepted and used testing procedures. Any new theory must account for what we have already been doing well. The difference the cybernetic approach will make is on the borders and in the directions in which testing for learning might expand. And *that* may make *all* the difference.

References

Campbell, Donald T. 1974. Evolutionary Epistemology. In *The Philosophy of Karl Popper,* Vol. 14, 1 and 2, *The Library of Living Philosophers,* P. A. Schilpp, ed. LaSalle, Ill.: Open Court.

Campbell, Donald T. 1959. Methodological Suggestions from a Comparative Psychology of Knowledge Processes. *Inquiry* 2:152:182.

Gronlund, Norman E. 1976. *Measurement and Evaluation in Teaching,* 3rd ed. New York: Macmillan.

Halstead, Robert E. 1975. Teaching for Understanding. *Phi-*

losophy of Education. Philosophy of Education Society, 52-62.

Kuhn, Thomas. 1974. Second Thoughts on Paradigms. In *The Structure of Scientific Theories,* Frederick Suppe, ed. Urbana, Ill.: University of Illinois Press.

Petrie, Hugh G. 1977. Comments on H. S. Broudy's "Types of Knowledge and Purposes of Education." In *Schooling and the Acquisition of Knowledge,* R. C. Anderson, R. J. Spiro, and W. E. Montague, eds. Hillsdale, N.J.: Lawrence Erlbaum Associates, 19-26.

Petrie, Hugh G. 1976. Metaphorical Models of Mastery: Or How to Learn to Do the Problems at the End of the Chapter in the Physics Textbook. In *PSA, 1974,* R. S. Cohen et al., eds. Dordrecht, Holland: D. Reidel, 301-312.

Petrie, Hugh G. 1974. Action, Perception, and Education. *Educational Theory* 24:33-45.

Petrie, Hugh G. 1971. Science and Metaphysics: A Wittgensteinian Interpretation. In *Essays on Wittgenstein,* E. Klemke, ed. Urbana, Ill.: University of Illinois Press, 106-121.

Powers, William T. 1973. *Behavior: The Control of Perception.* Chicago: Aldine.

Ryan, Alan. 1970. *The Philosophy of the Social Sciences.* New York: Pantheon.

Scriven, Michael. 1972. Objectivity and Subjectivity in Educational Research. In *Philosophical Redirection of Educational Research: The Seventy-first Yearbook of the National Society for the Study of Education,* Lawrence G. Thomas, ed. Chicago: National Society for the Study of Education.

Smith, Ralph, ed. 1975. *Regaining Educational Leadership: Essays Critical of PBTE/CBTE.* New York: Wiley.

Stake, Robert E. 1973. Measuring What Learners Learn. In *School Evaluation: The Politics and Process,* Ernest R. House, ed. Berkeley, Calif.: McCutchan, 193-223.

Toulmin, Stephen. 1972. *Human Understanding, Volume I.* Princeton, N.J.: Princeton University Press.

5
Cognitive-Developmental Assessment in Children: Application of a Cybernetic Model

Howard B. Gallas
Irving E. Sigel

Within a short space of time (about 3 to 4 years), the young child shows a remarkable set of transformations, aptly described by Flavell (1977, p. 71):

> It is hard to overemphasize just how radical a transformation the advent of these new abilities created in the life of the child and of those who interact with him. He becomes increasingly teachable, increasingly trainable, and . . . increasingly testable. He develops a measure of purposefulness in his daily activities at home and at school. He can sometimes inhibit a forbidden unwanted response, even though the response is prepotent and the temptation to let it go is very strong. He becomes a comprehending and comprehensible, governable and self-governing, internally guided and truly "voluntary" organism—and all that adds up to a radical transformation by anyone's standards.

Flavell's description poses an interesting question for us: namely, how do we conceptualize the child's "becoming" more trainable, more testable, more voluntary? Our contention is that the child "becomes" all of these as a direct result of a number of transformations within his or her self-regulatory system. Further, behavior comes more under the child's control as he or she acquires additional knowledge and more complex strategies that, in turn, facilitate the application of this knowledge.

This chapter addresses the issue of how this complex

transformation can be understood in the context of assessment by presenting an alternative model to one we believe is *au courant*—the child as a reactive subject in the assessment situation. Our thesis is that the conventional psychometric approach is basically influenced by the reactive model of the individual. Therefore, the first section of this chapter will address this issue and conclude with an advocation for a shift in concept to that of an active model paradigm. From this psycho-logic, an alternative approach to assessment will be suggested that in essence is analogous to a cybernetic model couched herewith in humanistic terms.

The Conventional Psychometric Model of Assessment

Traditionally, psychological assessment of children's intellectual functioning has focused on "getting to know" *what* the child knows. Most psychological intelligence tests (e.g., Stanford-Binet, Wechsler-Bellevue Scales, Bayley Scales of Infant Development, etc.) involve asking questions and/or posing problems to be solved. Such data provide an inventory of knowledge vis-à-vis the particular class of items employed. The usefulness of such information for predicting academic achievement, inferring intellectual competence, or defining intellectual status relative to peers, has been repeatedly documented in the research and clinical literature, and these efforts can be characterized as product-oriented (i.e., identifying and interpreting responses to a given set of predetermined questions).

In the last few years, there has been an increasing interest in the processes involved in cognitive functioning. The work of Piaget among others has stimulated interest in alternative models to psychometric intelligence assessment (Elkind, 1969; Piaget, 1967). Educators and clinicians have voiced some concern about the limited understanding of cognitive development and functioning obtained from such standardized tests. In spite of these protests, little if anything has been done either conceptually or empirically to remedy the problem.

Our contention is that, unfortunately, psychometric tests

have consistently included the model of man in an essentially stimulus-response framework—man as the reactor. To demonstrate the validity of this argument, let us begin with an analysis of the standard psychological assessment situation. Proceeding with this analysis, we shall make reference to the similarities of the standard psychological experiment, while demonstrating how each of these data gathering strategies appears to have the same methodological substructure—the human as a reactive organism.

In the standardized type of testing format, an implied assumption exists that valid and reliable data accrue when all the participants in these testing and experimental situations respond to the same stimuli. Furthermore, the testing situation is formal; an examiner poses a question to the subject, who in turn provides a response that the examiner duly notes and evaluates as right or wrong. The examiner then proceeds to another question having nothing to do with the previous one. For example, let us examine a typical dialogue from the Wechsler Adult Intelligence Scale (vocabulary test): the examiner says, "I want you to tell me the meanings of some words. Let us start with *bed*; what does bed mean?" The examiner assumes that the participant understands he is to give the meaning. Is that the same as asking what is a bed; what do you do with bed? Can "bed" be used as a verb as in *to bed* (a phrase used in 18th century as to bed down, which is not scored as such in the manual)? In any event, the participant gives an answer that he/she feels is "appropriate" to the question. Thus, a limited interactive process continues throughout this vocabulary test. The subject produces some definition as his response and the examiner proceeds to the next word. There is obviously no relationship between words (it is not a discourse), nor is there any context in which the word is used. The examiner only has to know whether the subject produced a response that is consistent with the manual's definition. Based on these standard definitions, a score is achieved for each response (i.e., verbal definition).

The items employed by the examiner are written in a manual with exact instructions for their presentation. The scoring is also fixed and the summed scores are subsequently used to create an index which is compared to a table of scores producing another index. All of this activity is in the service of standardization. The testing paradigm is based on the principle that controlling the administration of the test and the scoring are necessary so that each respondent's performance is accurately evaluated. Further, this evaluation of performance allows one to establish relationships for reference populations (normative). The implicit assumption is that subjects' responses are to identical stimuli. Thus variation in individual's responses, e.g., right or wrong, reflect individual differences in response to a common item. Again, the assumption is that there is an objective reality to which the subject is asked to respond, and that this reality is measurable and palpable. Indeed, the object/subject distinction is the basic paradigmatic perspective of the psychometric model.

Interestingly, this model of man underlying psychometrics is, in our judgment, similar to the one underlying experimental research in human behavior. Psychometric and laboratory research in human behavior is essentially based on the proposition that it is measurable and that responses can be meaningfully quantified. This measurement assumption reveals the close conceptual alignment of the behavioral sciences to the natural sciences. First, the paradigm of a subject or an object that is to be acted upon by some treatment is a bona fide characterization of the experiment in psychology. Indeed, this commonality is expressed in the scientific terminology, e.g., *standardization, measurement, control, prediction, manipulation, replication, subject, experimenter.* Each of these terms is equally applicable to natural science as well as behavioral science activity. Further, these concepts also connote a passive-reactive subject be it a child, a chemical, or some physical substance.

The aforementioned perspective reflects the classical Newtonian model of an ordered, predictable universe. However, the Newtonian view of the physical world has been shattered over the past 75 years with the development of the theory of relativity, the uncertainty principle, and the theory of complementarianism among others (Matson, 1964). For the physicists to speak of indeterminacy, to contend that even inorganic matter is not precisely predictable, and to raise serious doubts about the classical views of cause-effect accentuates the psychologists' dilemma. If inorganic matter cannot be precisely predicted and controlled, then what can be said about the human being who is not only more complex in structure and function, but also capable of purposeful and goal-directed actions? The call, therefore, is to evaluate the conceptual paradigm that guides psychological assessment and research.

If the human is conceptualized as a reactive organism, then the methodology employed in current research is reasonable and appropriate. The role of the experimenter or the assessor is to provide the particular stimulus and note the response. The tradition that guides these assessment and experimental procedures can be said, in the words of Matson (1964, p. 181), to derive "from the venerable tradition concerning the dichotomy of man and nature—more exactly the receptive organism and the impinging world. Because human beings in ordinary experience appeared all but powerless in the face of external forces, it seemed reasonable and plausible to give attention to the overriding impact of the environment upon man, rather than the puny actions of man upon the environment. Things and events 'out' there were the controlling factors and human behavior the passive and predictable response." However, the revolution in physics (psychologists' scientific ego ideal) that permeated the psychological community created a shift in focus which has continued to evolve —namely, conceptualizing the human as an active and purposive organism capable of regulating its own behavior, but also capable of functioning in a reactive, quasipassive way. In effect, the human has options in how to respond—actively and/or passively. The individual can accomplish this because he can control his own behavior—he can make decisions. With this in mind, let us turn to a consideration of the human as an active organism.

The Concept of the Active Organism and Its Derivatives

Space and purpose in this chapter preclude our detailing

how the various philosophers of science contributed to the erosion of the behavioristic-reactive model of man. Simply put, the intellectual climate reevaluated its view of man on the basis of developments in physics, coming to the realization that man, as a representative of living systems, "operates on two complementary levels. One level is that of mechanism, mechanical in process and mechanistic (physico-chemical) in analysis. The other level is *free from mechanism*, both in process and in observation" (Matson, 1964, p. 166). To be free from mechanisms implies freedom, to be in control, where control is voluntary, and by so doing to be free to pursue one's destiny. Thus, human behavior is a function of the two complementary principles.

Directing our attention to that aspect of the human being which functions free from mechanics, we now focus on psychological functioning. We hasten to add that there is no doubt that a relationship between the physico-system and the behavioral one exists. There is enough current data to demonstrate the existence of numerous relationships between brain functioning and behavior (Pribram, 1971). In spite of these interdependencies, there is also sufficient evidence, both anecdotal and research-based, to indicate that the individual is a self-directed, purposeful organism (Burtalanffy, 1968). In fact, historical analyses of martyrs and the history of warfare indicate that man is capable of behaviors that are counter to his innate physico-chemical mechanisms.

Therefore, to place our argument of the self-directed nature of human behavior in the context of the active organism is both logical and psychological. One of the manifestations of activity and self-direction is self-regulation.

The human organism is an open system that has the inherent capability of directing and monitoring its own behavior, making choices, and altering its direction in the service of its purposes (Bertalanffy, 1968).

Within this framework, let us examine two key concepts which are conceptually integral to an active organism perspective—self-regulation and feedback.

Self-Regulative Concept

Self-regulation or self-monitoring, in our conception, refers to voluntariness, and hence self-consciousness; that one's response is under one's control (even though not all elements of the response are under his control). For example, as one sits and writes, the light in the room may alter with con- comitant-noncomitant changes in pupil dilation. If, in spite of maximal dilation to accommodate a decrement in lighting, one decides that he cannot read any more, he must decide whether to turn on the lamp or stop writing. The latter are voluntary, self-regulatory actions while the former are based on physico-chemical features. This example ties together both physiological and psychological behaviors. In fact, behavior cannot occur without an array of physiological substrates. It is a matter of relative interdependence and influence as well as the degree of control of these physi- ological and psychological systems that defines voluntary control.

Self-regulation does not appear *de novo* or at a particular point in the child's life. Regulatory mechanisms are intrinsic to the developing and functional organism from birth. Regu- lations of the autonomic nervous system function in the service of adaptation and consequent survival. Heart rate or breathing, for example, increase as activity levels increase. These functions are built into the system, forming the proto- type of psychological relations. We are not asserting that autonomic regulation is a necessary and sufficient prerequi- site for later self-regulation; rather, we are saying that physical and psychological regulatory processes are intrinsic to the organism and necessary for its survival. The analogue, however, is that as regulatory mechanisms are necessary for biological survival, self- (psychological-) regulatory processes are necessary for social survival. Although it is not the central theme of this discussion, we acknowledge the importance of a basic understanding of how these self-regulatory mecha- nisms develop. From our perspective, we accept the fact that such mechanisms do exist and function in the service of adapting and coping with incoming stimulation. Therefore, we shall demonstrate how assessment and research with young children should utilize such an awareness.

Feedback Concept

For purposes of this discussion, feedback occurs when an individual assimilates knowledge and subsequently engages in self-correcting behaviors which alter any additional responses. Hence, the concept of feedback should be viewed as more than an outgrowth of a correct or incorrect response to a test question. Nonetheless, research which incorporates assessment techniques continues to evaluate a child's current body of knowledge solely on the basis of performance. This is not our conception of feedback, since knowledge of results is but an initial step in a more involved and complex process.

> A feedback control system incorporates three primary functions: it generates movement of the system toward a target or defined path; it compares the effects of this action with the true path and detects error; and it utilizes this error signal to redirect the system. . . . In the cybernetic analogy, the behaving individual is looked on as a control system which like a servo-mechanism generates a course of action and then redirects or corrects that action by means of feedback information (Smith and Smith, 1966, p. 203).

Using this description of a feedback process, it is quite evident that simply reviewing knowledge of results is insufficient for a complete understanding of environmental processing. An additional step of internally processing knowledge must follow for knowledge to function on a self-regulatory basis. Further, receipt of knowledge places the individual in a position to construct new strategies to adequately evaluate more complex tasks.

Each piece of information that an individual receives is processed in one of two ways. There can be an immediate association (almost reflexive in nature) where the response is virtually instantaneous. (For example, what is your name? What is your birth date?) In this case, there is instant retrieval. However, other types of inquiries or information involve reflection—interpreting or decoding the message and taking action in response to that information. Posing a mathematical question or an opinion question or presenting a novel problem requires the individual to employ previously accumulated and stored information to solve or cope with the new situation.

In addition, feedback can be viewed as both external and

internal. External feedback can best be explained when the individual is presented with the results of some query. This is often a deliberate procedure employed in experimentation in education. Another form of external feedback occurs when the individual is able to perceive consequences of his/her own behavior (e.g., an individual involved in a bowling tournament). Furthermore, information processing involves internal feedback during which the individual "internalizes" negative external feedback to avoid making an error, or stated in a positive sense, employs self-correction before answering the problem at hand. For example, asking a child a mathematical question involving relative rates of speed, posing an analogous question, comparing one set of items to another, or requesting the interpretation of a proverb involve (1) interpretation of the question or problem, (2) identification of the proper set of information relevant to that problem, (3) internal reflection of the response, (4) making the proper correction or inhibition of the seemingly wrong response, and finally (5) production of an answer. However, if this answer is wrong or the child senses that it is wrong, an opportunity exists for external feedback to set self-regulatory processes in motion; in other words, the circuitry is activated. In essence, we hold that external and internal feedback function in an interdependent way in problem-solving situations.

What the child is doing throughout these experiences is constructing and reconstructing new knowledge. The processes involved in these constructions incorporate both external and internal feedback systems. In this capacity, the child is developing higher ordered self-corrective internal and subsequently external actions.

Application of Feedback to the Assessment of Children

The child coming to the testing situation brings a repertoire of skills and knowledge that will be brought to bear on the demands of the immediate situation. The self-correcting adjustments made in that context will heavily depend on the developmental level of the child. The identification of this developmental level (the prime objective of this form of evaluation) can only be made through assessments which are extensive and intensive. Extensive assessment refers to determining the breadth of knowledge and/or skills, while intensive assessment refers to the quality and precision of that particular knowledge. For example, extensive assessment might ask the child to "tell me all the animals that live in the zoo," whereas an intensive question might require the child to "tell me how I know what an animal is." On the basis of these responses, the examiner attempts to establish the child's knowledge base. To determine the child's developmental level, an additional step is needed—a developmental characterization of performance. Currently there are few systematic conceptualizations of development with which to assess level. Piaget (1972a) and Werner (1948) present two systems that describe the quality and quantity of development. Each proposes a stage-like sequence of growth, wherein the child shifts progressively from a sensorimotor (action based) approach to a conceptual-logical and inferential approach as characteristic. Thus, according to conventional assessments with children, verification of where the child is in this progression is feasible.

As we shall show in our analysis, most of the traditional assessment research paradigms fail to produce data that explicitly allow for level determination. It might be argued that if this assertion is true, the developmental progression is invalid. Our argument is that the validity of these stages is questioned because their identification is a function of a diverse variety of research paradigms, few of which accurately tap the young child's developmental level or stage. Further, at every stage of development the child constructs additional knowledge through the use of cognitive-perceptual mechanisms employing attention, memory, and subsequent retrieval strategies to deal with novel situations. Unfortunately, no one has yet adequately tapped the developmental changes that take place in these constructs during early childhood.

According to Piaget, knowledge acquired through experience is organized into schemata. These include a variety of information bits which cohere because of their interdependence.

Figure 1

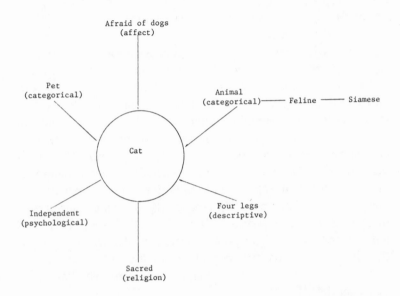

N.B. This is but a skeleton schema of the large number of attributes that can be incorporated into the "cat" schema. The reader can fill in his/her own additions. It is readily observable how extensive an array of attributes can characterize the cat.

Examination of Figure 1 will help illustrate the schema concept. The concept "cat" is the nucleus of our schemata. A cat can be defined in a variety of ways—in terms of its physical characteristics, functional/behavioral attributes, class membership, relation to other animals or objects. These bits of knowledge are, in a sense, organized. If asked "what is a cat?" the response would be linear and unidirectional (i.e., a single utterance). Traditional assessment procedures code that particular "knowledge level." (For example the response "animal" may be coded as more conceptual than the response "four legged.") The total knowledge and the relationship of the emitted information to the entire schema of cat will not be known to the assessor. How or why the child selected and verbalized a particular term from his or her cognitive data bank is also unknown. It is evident, however, that the paradigm used in this assessment situation has elicited a single response uttered in a single moment providing no opportunity for any self-correcting response.

While the previous example was drawn from the verbal domain, tasks that involve self-corrective procedures such as solving maze problems or building requested block formations, do not use the data generated from the child's self-corrective behaviors even though they are necessitated in standardized assessments. Therefore, the active organism model of human development must call for a more encompassing model of assessment—a cybernetic model. This is because a cybernetic model is essentially a feedback model involving internal regulators which govern responsivity. In fact, Piaget (1973, p. 527) eloquently describes the appropriateness in these words: "It [cybernetics model] is . . . a natural to use. . . . The great advantage of such a model is that it makes it possible to analyze constituent processes and *not just* the results or performance as is often the case with other models."

The assessment procedure employed by Piaget to analyze the constituent processes is similar to the clinical interview employed by psychiatrists as a means of diagnosis. The method is called "méthode clinique," i.e., clinical method. It is experimental "in one sense that the practitioner sets himself a problem, makes hypotheses, adapts the conditions to them and finally controls each hypothesis by testing it against the reactions he stimulates in conversation" (Piaget, 1972b, p. 8).

This method of interview is our choice for intellectual assessment in children since the examiner is working with a *feedback* model, constructing his concepts of the child and reconstructing them on the basis of feedback relative to the child's performance on a given task or set of tasks. The interviewer is not the only active, constructing participant in this model of the evaluation situation. The examiner's actions and reactions are intimately related to the child who is being interviewed. After the interviewer poses a problem, e.g., "What makes the sun move?" the child, possessing similar organismic characteristics as the interviewer, interprets each question and then proceeds to give an answer. This is the opening gambit of a series of interactions between the interviewer and the interviewee. Hence, there are feedback loops operating for both the interviewer and for the child. Momentarily, we shall consider the contingencies of these feedback loops.

Before proceeding with a detailed example of the clinical method, let us clarify two important issues. First, every test attempts, as we said, to evaluate what the respondent knows. If the sole purpose of the interview is to determine *what* knowledge the interviewee possesses, then items of a convergent type are useful. (For example, to learn if the individual has a particular bit of historical knowledge, a question such as, "When did Columbus discover America?" or "When is George Washington's birthday?" is appropriate.) On the other hand, if the evaluation is designed to discover *how* an individual thinks and how certain is he of that knowledge, the conventional method is not, in our opinion, desirable since it does not allow us to examine which processes are involved in solving the problem.

The Clinical Method Approach to Assessment *

Where the selection of the problem is based on relevant epistemological grounds, the individual child utilizes and applies his own cognitive apparatus. The task for the interviewer is to obtain reliable and trustworthy data. This is indeed an uncertain situation in contrast to conventional tests which usually pose a highly structured, precise question, leaving the respondent little choice in *how* to answer. The burden for the clinical interviewer is to know how to carry out not only a careful inquiry but also a careful evaluation of the respondent's explanations. Piaget has said,

*This section appeared in a paper by I.E. Sigel and R. R. Cocking, "A Cybernetic Approach to Psychological Testing of Children," presented at the meeting of the American Association for the Advancement of Science, Denver, Colorado, February 1977. It is to be published in *Cybernetics Forum* and is reprinted here with the permission of that journal. For details on the clinical method, see Piaget, 1972b, pp. 1-32.

The greatest enemies of the clinical methods are those who unduly simplify the results of an interrogatory, those who either accept every answer the child makes as pure gold or those on the
other hand who class all as dross. The first, naturally, are the more
dangerous, but both fall into the same error, that is, of supposing
that everything a child may say during a quarter, half or three-
quarters of an hour of conversation, lies on the same psychological level—that of considered belief, for example (Piaget, 1972b,
p. 9).

The first caveat proposed by Piaget is that the examiner
listen to the response which serves as data (feedback), so that
he can order (regulate) subsequent questions to obtain the
relevant information. Concurrently, the examiner is actively
constructing the child's response, forming and reformulating
hypotheses about the child's cognitive status.

The child, recipient of the problem, provides a solution
which the examiner must evaluate: does the answer fit the
examiner's expectations? Is the child's response the child's
conviction or does it reflect his/her submission to the
authority of the adult examiner? Rules for classifying the
child's response and procedures for evaluating the intensity
or solidity of the child's conviction must be created. One
method of testing the solidity of a conviction is the use of
a counter suggestion. A second method is to pose the same
problem in another context or in a potently contradicting
way.

While the examiner is engaged in gathering information
that influences his subsequent interrogation, the child is also
gathering information. The child is presented with a problem
he probably never thought about in any active way (e.g.,
"What makes the sun move?"). Presented with such a question, the child probably invents an answer. This invention
occurs during the inquiry, but an answer does not arise *sui
generis*. Piaget (1972b, p. 13) points out that such answers,
"imply previously formed schemas, tendencies of the mind,
intellectual habits." The child's response influences the examiner's subsequent inquiry, and if he is a skilled interviewer, he
will avoid suggesting an answer. The very fact that the child's
response does not terminate the inquiry is conjectured as

having a direct effect on the child's construction of the situation.

Feedback from the testing situation occurs at two points. The first occurs when the child becomes aware of *his* answer to a novel question, since he had to transform the inquiry into a verbal reply. This may pose a problem as it is possible that the child does not possess an adequate vocabulary to clearly express himself to the adult (examiner). This internal act of transformation is *feedback* with the constraints defined by both the child's language comprehension and usage levels. Since his response immediately results in a follow-up question from the interviewer, a second set of messages is possible. To wit, did he (the child) give the right answer and did the interviewer understand, etc. In turn, an additional feedback situation is established—an interaction between the examiner and the child. Each participant's behavior is contingent on the behavior of the other and also contingent on the prior set of questions. In other words, once the inquiry is set in motion, each answer influences the subsequent interviewer-child interactions. In the following example, consider each statement, first for its independence.

Teacher: How are a cat and a dog alike?

Child: They both have legs?

T: Any other way they are alike?

C: They both have whiskers?

T: If I see a man with whiskers and legs does this make him a dog or a cat?

C: No. A man has two legs and a dog and cat have four legs.

T: I thought you said a dog and cat are alike because they have legs.

C: Oh yes, but they have the same number of legs. That is how they are alike.

T: Then if a man has whiskers and four legs could he be like a dog or a cat?

C: No. A man does not have four legs.

T: But he has legs.

C: Yes.

T: Does the number of legs make a difference?

C: Oh, I see. A dog, a cat and a man have legs. That is how they are alike. But a dog and cat have four legs and a man has only two. That is how the man is different.

T: Then the cat and the dog and the man are alike in some ways and different too.

C: Yes.

This interview segment reveals how the teacher continues to probe the child's knowledge of attributes common to a dog and cat. By including a contrary example, the teacher confronts the child with a contradiction. Getting such feedback from the teacher, we believe, contributes to differentiation and also highlights that the concept of "legness" is distinct from number of legs. The child makes the connection and now is responding in a hierarchical way—i.e., the class "legness" contains a subset of items defined by the number of legs.

It is easy to see that neither the answers nor the questions are independent. This example illustrates the interdependence of the feedback loops for both the examiner and the child. It is also interesting to note the interdependence or relatedness of answers that exist for the child—the child's self-regulated loop. This protocol demonstrates how the examiner probes the issue and how the child continues in his own way, unaware of the contradiction in his statement. Further, this protocol suggests that the child may not use his own information as feedback to alter his conviction that a cat and a dog are alike because they have legs, but a man is not like them even though he has legs. The implicit idea that the child did not mention is that the number of legs is a critical feature. The child's responses are influenced during inquiry conceivably influencing the organization of his cognitive structure.

For the model we are presenting, it is possible and even probable that a feedback looping exists between questions; that is, each response made by the child is contingent upon the previous inquiry and previous response. In fact, this interrogatory model is widely discussed among communication researchers (Mishler, 1975). The contingencies established when an adult is in control of the conversation produce a chaining effect of *Question*, followed by an *Answer* which is dependent upon the *Question*, which in turn is followed by another *Question* that is dependent upon the *Answer*, and so forth. However, experienced interviewers also acknowledge that children often impose their own questions onto the conversation; thus the dialogue takes on a very different form. When the respondent and the interviewer simultaneously use questions an "arching" occurs. The child often does this to clarify something that the examiner has asked and usually the exchange quickly resumes in a "chaining" format. The interrogatory model becomes a feedback teaching/learning model since the conversation is extended through the use of questions. This set of circular reactions proceeds until the interviewer or the child terminates the discussion.

The implications of this analysis are: (1) conventional testing appears to treat the child as a relatively passive respondent whose answers to decontextualized information are assumed to reflect mental status; (2) while acknowledging the usefulness of such information regarding children's intellectual abilities, the traditional approach deemphasizes the active engagements, constructions, and regulatory processes continually involved in both individuals during the testing situation. Consequently, a clinical method appears more consistent with the previously outlined organismic characteristics; and (3) the application of the clinical method as described allows for a more comprehensive statement of the child's intellectual level on both qualitative and quantitative planes.

One could argue that an open-ended assessment approach mixes models and therefore is inconsistent. This is not the case. Two basic functions undergird the diagnostic effort: (1) the attempt to understand how the child functions cognitively, and (2) the quantity of information that the child has available within several domains. Each of these functions allows for differential predictive power. Understanding how a child thinks, reasons, and the processes employed in problem-solving yields a qualitative statement reflecting the child's cognitive-perceptual capabilities. On the basis of data so gathered, inferences can be made regarding subsequent functioning. However, such predictions can only be made within the context of a system of development. Simply knowing how the child functions is insufficient to make definitive statements regarding subsequent functioning *in toto*. In this instance, it is important to determine to what kind of situation or to what kind of task one is predicting.

Too often predictions are made out of context. To learn, for example, that a child is capable of hierarchical classification and that he is able to understand how to integrate new information suggests that he will also understand and assimilate any and all information dealing with biological classification; in other words, he can come to terms with the problem of classifying particular animals in some order although specific information may not be available to him. To further illustrate this point, the child may not know what a pterodactyl dinosaur is, a bird or a reptile. Yet, the processes involved will permit him to deal with the task since *they are* available. It is our contention that predictions of cognitive behavior are enhanced to the degree that the situation is predefined in a given behavioral context. On the other hand, when there is no definition to the outcome situation, prediction will be of a very low order of accuracy. With respect to product information, predictions are once more possible. Again, the same principle holds; namely, the knowledge level identified will act as a base for subsequent predictions when situations require such knowledge. For example, a child's knowledge of the multiplication tables should predict to the child's solving of multiplication problems.

Conclusion

Typically, assessment procedures are employed to diagnose the current or predicted behaviors (status) of the participant. The clinical method is most appropriate if the tester wishes to uncover the competence and performance levels of the child and the strategies that he or she is capable of employing.

If, on the other hand, one's intent is to identify what the child knows—a useful approach for some educational purposes—then more traditional assessment procedures are in order. Therefore, we encourage further exploration of the issues that surface in viewing the organism as an active participant during assessment procedures in a given context. Depending upon the nature of the data sought about a child, an additional option, for example, is to use a dialogue to explore more intensively the cognitive processes of the child than is possible with the standard testing approach. The form of the dialogue (an interactive system) would represent an experience in which there is evidence of feedback between the child and the interviewer. We conclude by stating that conscious flexibility in the incorporation of these assessment procedures would provide a broader base-assessment of processes and a more coherent understanding of the young child's cognitive capabilities as they are developing.

References

Bertalanffy, L. von. 1968. *General Systems Theory.* New York: George Braziller.
Elkind, D. 1969. Piagetian and Psychometric Conceptions of Intelligence. *Harvard Educational Review* 39, no. 2, pp. 319-337.
Flavell, J. H. 1977. *Cognitive Development.* Englewood Cliffs, N.J.: Prentice-Hall.
Matson, F. W. 1964. *The Broken Image.* New York: George Braziller.
Mishler, E. G. 1975. Studies in Dialogue and Discourse: II. Types of Discourse Initiated by and Sustained Through Questioning. *Journal of Psycholinguistic Research* 4, no. 2, pp. 99-121.
Piaget, J. 1967. Genesis and Structure in the Psychology of Intelligence. In D. Elkind, ed. *Six Psychological Studies by Jean Piaget.* New York: Random House, pp. 147-158.
Piaget, J. 1972a. *Psychology of Intelligence.* Totowa, N.J.: Littlefield, Adams & Co.
Piaget, J. 1972b. *The Child's Conception of the World.*

Totowa, N.J.: Littlefield, Adams & Company.

Piaget, J. 1973. *Main Trends in Psychology.* New York: Harper & Row.

Pribram, K. H. 1971. *Languages of the Brain.* Englewood Cliffs, N.J.: Prentice-Hall.

Smith, K. V., and Smith, M. F. 1966. *Cybernetic Principles of Learning and Educational Design.* New York: Holt, Rinehart & Winston.

Werner, H. 1948. *Comparative Psychology of Mental Development.* Chicago, Ill.: Follett Publishing Company.

Part 3

The Application of Cybernetics
to the Assessment of Children

6
New Directions in the Assessment of Children's Language

Rodney R. Cocking

The topic of this chapter is language assessment. Language is here restricted to the structural features that can be subjected to formal testing. Other aspects of language, such as communication, semantics, and so forth, are not considered less important, but the central issues in language assessment can be illustrated adequately with recourse only to grammatical features. *Language* is going to have another restriction on its meaning in this paper: I intend to present the case for assessment in such a way as to imply that language means "language knowledge." I want to present a type of knowledge that is assessed when we test children's grammatical development. I also wish to be consistent with Piagetian principles, which indicate that the types of knowledge essential to general cognitive functioning consist of more than accumulations, accretions, and acquisitions of information. In this sense, we will be discussing *organizations* of information.

Piaget states that organization and regulation are processes that the individual himself uses; they are autoregulatory control systems. The most basic type of autoregulation that Piaget discusses is assimilation, a feedback process whereby all new experience is brought into an existing framework or structure. The feedback model, however, is not linear as in trial-and-error, chained learning; rather, it is cyclical. Circular reactions are a means for feedback of not only external stimuli, but also of organismic information to be included in the sensory integration process that occurs during assimilation. In this sense, Piaget (1971, p. 61) says that his model of human behavior includes mechanisms for directing oneself and others "by means of retroactive or anticipatory effects of information given."

The processes of self-regulation and other-regulation are predicated on *reconstructive* and *anticipatory* cognitive functions. *Reconstructions* involve the remembering and assembling of previous experiences. *Anticipations* extend these past experiences toward future expectations. In each of these processes, the information from the past is retained, or conserved, and aids in the regulation of ongoing behavior. Piaget (1971, p. 61) states that anticipation is "an extention of all forms of conserved information," illustrating how very basic these regulatory mechanisms are to cognition.

How are these processes expressed in behaviors? Specifically, how are they reflected in *language* behaviors? Descriptive, reconstructive, anticipatory, and evaluative language behaviors are the classes of linguistic structures that fit the cybernetic model Piaget proposes. The issues that have to be resolved to answer our question revolve around how to gather linguistic data from children to test the model, deciding on the proper unit of analysis for reducing those data, and determining the validity of such evaluation. Two general approaches to answering the question will be the subject of this chapter.

Language is generally studied as developmental *products*. Measuring what a subject knows at Time 1, at Time 2, etc., and the changes that occur over time, is the way to evaluate children's language. What these procedures have told us about language as a cognitive product will be presented in the first portion of the chapter.

The final section of the chapter will present the second approach to answer the question about how regulatory processes are reflected in language behavior. This second view is not concerned so much with mapping the milestones of linguistic development as with children's language usage. So, the second portion of the chapter will discuss language behaviors as they are employed by children for regulating behaviors—their own behaviors and the behaviors of others. Awareness of the principles of both autoregulation and social regulation, then, will be the focus for applying a feedback model to language measurement.

Assessment Measures

Validity and Valid Units of Measurement in Evaluating Children's Language

In a 1975 article, Sigel examined the measurement problem in early childhood education and questioned the adequacy of measurement on two basic points. The first problem concerns the validity of measurement. The second involves determining the proper *unit of measurement.*

In language research, the fundamental problem is the validity of measurement. For productive or expressive language, the issue is the validity of the instruments used for assessing children's grammatical development and the syntactic complexities in verbal expressions. Generally, the measurement issue is phrased in terms of a question such as "How should we assess the *complexity* of the child's language?" Here "language" means the ostensible, verbal production that the child is capable of generating himself.

To determine the validity of measurement we must first find a respectable index of validity. If we choose concurrent validity, we concern ourselves with finding related, appropriate language instruments to confirm the results of our new instrument. Generally, tests that have been in the literature for a long time, such as the Peabody Picture Vocabulary Test (PPVT), are used for supportive evidence. If we follow Piaget's theory, a test that reflects understanding, such as the language comprehension test designed by Bellugi-Klima (1971), might be selected.

Concurrent validity is not always the best index for establishing validity, however. In fact, concurrent validity is an inappropriate index for language production. This judgment is based on the developmental histories of the behaviors that the validation instruments assess. Instruments utilized to corroborate the new data are often based on language skills that have a different developmental history from the acquisition of syntax. For example, we wouldn't evaluate children's walking skills with a crawling test; they are independent behaviors, related only by their developmental sequence. Concurrent validity requires the use of a task that measures the *same* behavior as the original task. Usually the tests selected for validating language production instruments are not appropriate because they measure different aspects of related behaviors. The Peabody Picture Vocabulary Test, for instance, measures the child's lexicon. The child may label a picture with a word without expressing any of the structural features of language. He doesn't have to produce a fully formed simple or transformed sentence when he points to a picture of a "hot dog" or a "butterfly" or to a "thermometer" when the tester asks him to point to the picture "that best shows temperature." That task is very different from constructing a grammatically correct—or even a grammatically imperfect— statement.

Some form of language comprehension is a second type of task frequently used to establish concurrent validity for language production. Bellugi's tasks, for example, involve asking children to manipulate objects in accordance with tester requests. When the syntactic class assessed is that of prepositions, for example, the child is told to put the ball in, on top of, beside, etc., a cup. The problem with this kind of validation instrument for production data resides in a developmental discrepancy between these two types of behaviors. That is, for fairly parallel structures, language comprehension characteristically precedes production, often by six or more months. For some structures, however, production may lag several years behind the comprehension of the material (Cocking and Potts, 1976; Chomsky, 1969).

The question then becomes, "Where do we go to validate our procedures for collecting information about children's language usage if concurrent validity is inappropriate?" A common approach is to compare language test behavior with naturalistic samples of children's speech under standard conditions in a variety of contexts. This solution brings us to the second point Sigel alluded to—the specification of the units of measurement. The definition of these units is inextricably related to the issue of valid measurement. What I wish to point out for the following discussion is that the selection of criteria for evaluating children's speech in naturalistic settings is no simple task. I will briefly review several different approaches for evaluating free-speech samples. These represent the most common procedures, but in actuality there are numerous other, less common approaches.

In an earlier study (Cocking and Potts, 1974) we undertook an analysis to determine the best indicators of "complexity" for evaluating speech samples. For those analyses we considered that we could look at the *amount* of verbalizing by the children or the *varieties* of ways for coding syntactic classes present in the samples. Even for within-sentence analyses there were various ways to determine sentence *complexities* and word-*structure* analyses. We studied 19 four-year-olds on each of these four variables by using free-speech, naturalistic samples from Head Start children as each engaged in discussions of toy descriptions and usages with an experimenter. The subjects' command of various forms of syntax was evaluated with the Test of Syntactic Productions (Potts, 1972).

The purpose of this chapter is not to discuss all of the interrelationships among these procedures, but let me briefly outline what each of the procedures showed us about children's language.

Total verbalization. The total amount of verbalization from these protocols was the most obvious way for dealing with free-speech samples from children. The assumption is that the number of sentences children utter is in some way related to how well they can talk. The index is easily obtained by counting the number of sentences emitted during an observation.

Adjusted total output. This is a variation on the "total sentence output" procedure; the "total number of sentences score" is adjusted. Whereas the first method utilizes a score based on the entire sentence output, this second type of score is adjusted to eliminate (1) repetitions and (2) imitations the child makes of others present (such as the tester's remarks).

Each of these methods, when correlated with a test of language production, yields a nonsignificant coefficient. The number of syntactic structures a child is capable of producing in a test situation, therefore, is not related to the *quantity* of verbal output in a free-speech assessment.

Mean Length of Utterance. Two additional methods for dealing with free-speech samples are probably the most commonly used procedures, being derived from the ever-popular Mean Length of Utterance (MLU) index. Brown (1973, p. 110) has written the following about the merits of this procedure.

> The mean length of utterance is a good index of grammatical development because for several years practically everything the child learns about the structure of his language has the effect of increasing the length of his sentences. Mean length of utterance is a better index of level of grammatical development because there is substantial individual variation in the rate of development.

The first of these two procedures is a direct outgrowth of the total sentence output already discussed. In lieu of counting the total number of sentences, it became common practice to count the number of words per sentence and then to use the average as the index of grammatical development.

A second refinement of the MLU method was to substitute independent clauses for sentences and morphemes for words in deriving an index. The result was a score reflecting the number of morphemes per clause. The clause was used as the denominator in this ratio, replacing the sentence, to produce a smaller and more manageable unit, and also because of the difficulty of deciding what constitutes a "sentence" for young children whose sentences may be joined by a succession of "and . . . and . . . and." Similarly, since words are a reflection of vocabulary not linguistic structure, morphemes, as the basic unit of meaning, were selected as the numerator. The index, then, was a reflection of the amount of grammatical meaning contained in each clause.

The correlation between MLU and the test of syntactic production was about +5.4 for four-year-olds. Since morphological features are the most salient dialect variations one encounters in Head Start populations, it is not surprising that the correlation between test behavior and a situation in which the child can freely use his own dialect is low. The major drawback of MLU is its inappropriateness for evaluating speech of children who do not use a standard form of English. Second, and as we would suspect, the length of utterance increases with age, but only up to certain limits. In early language acquisition new morphemes reflect syntactic maturity, but after most sentence elements have entered the repertoire, the number of words or morphemes in a sentence or in a clause is no longer an adequate reflection of syntactic maturity. Shriner (1967) reports that children are not consistent in mean length of response from day to day, and therefore the technique is not a reliable procedure. While MLU is generally taken as a rough index of syntactic maturity, Menyuk (1971) points out that it provides merely a surface description of linguistic maturation. Perhaps a better index of complexity is one that focuses upon sentence features such as the complexities of the independent clause, rather than the word-related features of morphemes.

Because the mean is regarded by many to be subject to error, the mean length of utterance may be unduly affected by a few, atypically long or short sentences. The *Median Length of Utterance* is an additional unit for summarizing free-speech data. Researchers who have opted for this unit, however, have done so without reporting the actual gains in accuracy over the MLU.

Clauses per Terminal-Unit. Another procedure is an outgrowth of the notion of analyzing the independent clause as the unit of children's free speech. The number of clauses per sentence may be taken as an index of the *complexity* of children's language. Although "complexity" is generally the ideal way to evaluate development (assuming that there is a straightforward relationship between the embeddedness ·in children's sentences and general language development), the correlation between test performance (syntactic maturity) and the number of clauses per terminal-unit (clauses/T-unit) was about .27 for both four- and five-year-olds.

Evidence from free-speech protocols. Three additional procedures for evaluating naturalistic speech and its relationships with test performance involve straightforward searches through the complete tape-recorded protocols to determine if certain syntactic structures on the test also appear in the free-speech protocols.

The arduous task one encounters here, and the reason we evolved three different scoring systems within this procedure, is deciding on a criterion of "knowing" on the part of the child. We considered the following:

1. Does one occurrence constitute knowledge? The argument is made by some that the child couldn't produce the form without knowing it.
2. Others maintain a somewhat more rigorous criterion by insisting that, within the constraints on where a certain structure *ought* to be produced (saying "feet" instead of "foots"), the child must produce it correctly in 50 percent of situations where it is required.
3. The most rigorous criterion, of course, is to consider only a correct usage greater than 50 percent as acceptable.

In our study, we found that each of these free-speech criteria related to production test performance in the following way among the four-year-old Head Start enrollees.

One correct sample   +.49
Correct usage at least 50% of the time   +.67
Correct usage more than 50% of the time +.59

While one generally believes that the more rigorous the criterion he uses, the better the prediction, one can see here that there is not a great deal of variation between correct usage half of the time and correct usage more than half of the time.

Summary

The issue for discussion has been the concept of validity in assessing children's language. We concluded that concurrent validity, as frequently employed, is imperfect because of the different developmental patterns that exist between the validating instruments and the new methods being studied. Our examples were tests that tap the child's lexical development or language comprehension for validating language production. Neither is appropriate.

The use of free speech samples for determining test validity served to focus our attention on the units of measurement. For this purpose we considered methods that attend to the following aspects of language utterances: the quantity of verbal output; the morphological complexities of the words employed; the complexities of the clauses in children's sentences; and protocol searches for *a priori* syntactic categories.

The results indicate that extensive data-gathering efforts as required by free speech do not always pay off by giving the child the rare opportunity for uttering a profound and complex statement that might have been lost in a shorter test session. A correlation of -.04 between test production and amount of verbal output vividly illustrates that increased numbers of sentences do not necessarily increase the probability that a child will use a particular grammatical structure. It is also important to emphasize the relationship between the structures produced in a test situation and those generated in free speech. While the -.04 correlation indicates that we cannot expect sheer *quantities* of data to produce additional information, it is important to look at the processes and structures a child is using across situations. Correlations of +.49, +.67, and +.59 (for one correct usage, 50 percent correct usage, or greater than 50 percent usage, respectively) all indicate better prediction than *quantity* (total output) of verbalizing per se. However, in none of these accounts of validation criteria is the concept of feedback to the subject explicit.

The reason that feedback is never used in naturalistic speech sampling is that the observer would be guilty of altering the speech, that is, of influencing the data. Is the precaution necessary? We have seen that sheer amounts of verbal data from the children do not mean that the experimenter gets a better approximation of the speech categories by not intervening. We have also seen that whether the child, in a naturalistic setting, gives the structure correctly once in half of the situations where he uses it, or almost all of the time, doesn't make much difference in relation to test behavior. Modeling, or imitation procedures are perhaps the only feedback methods employed in naturalistic sampling. The object of these studies was not to sample speech acts, but rather to modify children's error patterns as they were spontaneously emitted. How successful are these kinds of feedback in modifying the child's language? McNeill (1966) cites the following example to illustrate the impenetrability of young children's language.

Child: Nobody don't like me.
Mother: No, say "nobody likes me."
Child: Nobody don't like me.

(eight repetitions of this dialogue)

Mother: No, now listen carefully; say *"nobody likes me."*
Child: Oh! Nobody don't likes me.

In Piagetian theory, the concept of feedback rides on a delicate balance, especially with regard to information which comes from others. Piaget points out that the organism must be sufficiently mature to be able to benefit from the incoming information. The information cannot be too advanced or difficult for assimilation nor so simple as to be uninteresting.

The complexity of feedback is even greater when social factors become involved. When regulation comes from external sources, other factors operate, factors such as the age of the child. Age is a particularly important factor, since young children operate principally on autoregulatory control processes and not on feedback from others. Social regulation has been shown (Cocking and Potts, 1975) to be an effective modifier of somewhat older children's linguistic behavior, but again the effect interacted with such other variables as the sex of the child and the age of the model. Feedback, in that study, was shown to be effective when it emanated from peers for the preschool boys and from adults for the girls.

Let us now turn to another feedback source in language assessment: the materials.

The Context of Assessment

Pictures and Objects in Assessing Children's Language

In the preceding discussion we looked at the interrelationships among the various indices of language behaviors. We will now shift to how children's language performance on tests can vary under differing test conditions. For this discussion, we will look at the response differences that can be attributed to the assessment materials. Specifically, we will investigate the differences betweeen objects and pictures of objects as test stimuli.

Children's performances on sorting tasks have consistently confirmed that it is more difficult to sort and make categories of pictures of objects than it is to make classifications of the actual objects (Sigel and McBane, 1967). The effect is independent of the children's abilities to recognize or to name either the objects or the depicted objects. This relatively greater difficulty of pictorial materials has been shown to be particularly strong within American subculture populations (Gray and Klaus, 1965; Sigel, Anderson, and Shapiro, 1966; Wysocki and Wysocki, 1969). Cross-cultural replications have similarly supported the picture-object discrepancy (Deregowski and Serpell, 1971).

It might therefore be expected that such a discrepancy affects children's performances in assessment tasks. Children's language development is a particularly common example of assessment procedures that use both pictures and objects. Bellugi-Klima (1971), for example, reports a comprehension assessment technique utilizing objects, while Brown (1957) used pictures for tapping comprehension. Potts (1972) reports a technique for production assessment, employing pictures in a story-completion format. Berko (1958) also used pictures in her morpheme test. Reynell

(1969) uses both pictures and objects in her assessment of expressive language; objects are used for the comprehension portion, and pictures in the content portion. It is only in the vocabulary section that objects and pictures are both employed. In spite of all these assessment tools, however, no studies report the effects of a possible picture-object discrepancy in their comparisons of the subjects' performances on production and comprehension tasks.

The evidence seems to imply easier task demands by object stimuli and by comprehension tasks, but a study was designed to look at the specific effects of picture and object stimuli on two types of language performance (Cocking and McHale, 1977).

Subjects were 48 white, four- and five-year-old, middle-class children from suburban communities, divided into four age groups of equal size, with each group evenly divided by sex. Groups were matched on the basis of age (within three months) and sex.

Four different tasks were administered, one to each group of children. The tasks varied across two dimensions: medium of the stimulus and type of response. Children were asked to respond to stories depicted by objects or pictures and the responses elicited were either verbal production responses or language comprehension responses. The tasks themselves assessed children's knowledge of 44 syntactic categories, tested across 100 items. Thus, the four tasks measured language comprehension using object stimuli, language production using object stimuli, comprehension with picture stimuli, and production with picture stimuli.

The object stimuli, toys, included two male and two female dolls as the subjects of most of the stories, as well as various props (balls, animals, cars, sticks, blocks, and dishes) to illustrate certain actions. For the tasks in the picture mode, black and white line drawings were presented on 21 x 27 cm cards. For the comprehension task, several picture choices were presented on a single card for each of the items. The pictures of the production task illustrated the stories presented verbally by the experimenter which S was to help complete. Each child was tested individually on one of the four tasks.

The results of the study indicated that four- and five-year-old children show overall superior performance on object-assessment tasks, compared to performance on picture-assessment tasks. I would like to suggest two reasons: the first dealing with children's understanding of pictorial representations, and the second with their acceptance of pictorial conventions. First, when a task depends directly upon the use and interpretation of pictures, it is assumed that all children have comparable abilities for decoding pictures for the message necessary to participate in the assessment. Such an assumption is not valid. There are individual differences in both picture decoding and picture comprehension abilities (Mackworth, 1972). Children can tell you what is in a picture without necessarily telling you what the picture means. Second, Cazden (1972, p. 263) has pointed out that correct interpretations of pictures may also depend upon "*acceptance* of particular conventions" (our emphasis). The acceptance of these conventions can influence the ways in which children respond to the task stimuli. Chittenden (1970), for example, analyzed stimuli and found that lower-socioeconomic and middle-socioeconomic-status children have different interpretations for some of the same pictures. Others (cited in Cazden, 1972, p. 264) have shown that these different interpretations can influence the children's responses to pictures—e.g., the shading convention of graphics was variously interpreted as light shadows or as dirt or a depiction of "dirty." Thus, children probably respond differentially to tasks that employ pictures.

It was also determined in this study that language comprehension tasks are performed more accurately than language production tasks among the four- and five-year-olds. The interactions, further, indicated that when pictures are used, children do significantly better on the comprehension task than on the production task, but the difference does not appear when objects are used. When assessing comprehension performance, it did not make a significant difference whether pictures or objects were used, but it did on the production task.

The results of this study demonstrate that when a task demand of comprehension or production is combined with the additional demand to make inferences based on the stimuli, the more difficult of the two language functions (production) is seriously affected, while the developmentally easier of the two (comprehension) remains unaffected.

Both of the concepts we are discussing, autoregulatory feedback processes and social-regulation feedback, are present in these findings. The control systems that permit assimilation to occur are, first of all, directed by interal controls. Comprehension strategies are present prior to generative strategies for most English structures, a feature of cognitive development. When externally discrepant information is imposed, such as the object-picture difference, the information for feedback to children who have already assimilated the comprehension schemes (as have most four- to five-year-olds), can be attended to without further distraction from the task demand. However, when this externally imposed task demand is to generate a structure to which the child has not yet accommodated, the only feedback device is in the materials themselves. When the child has to make inferences about object attributes from pictures of the objects, the external task demand goes beyond his assimilation capacities. The child, at this point, has neither anticipatory nor reconstructive assimilation recourse.

Let us now turn our attention to the implications of the first two sections of this chapter and consider how they bear on one another. I want to carefully look at two things: naturalistic speech sampling and the nature of the assessment materials. Can the problematic areas I pointed out for each of these issues be solved in some mutually efficacious way? The next section expores the usefulness of children's speech interactions about meaningful materials in a naturalistic setting.

The Small Group as a Source
for Naturalistic Language Samples *

Labov (1970) has discussed the peer group as a situation for

*The work reported in this section of the chapter describes, in part, a collaborative project conducted at Educational Testing Service in the Center for Child Care Research. Dr. Carol E. Copple was my colleague in this joint project. Funds were made available from a DHEW Biomedical Research Support Grant, No. 1-S07-RR05729-02.

eliciting linguistically rich and valid speech samples from
adolescents and preadolescents. He also discusses the need to
establish a relevant topic in these groups and to remove communication barriers by letting the participants know that
whatever they say is legitimate, including socially taboo
words. Labov's technique has two primary features that
should operate across all small groups for gathering language
samples. First, the motivational variable of having a meaningful topic to discuss means that conversations are not con-
strained by a participant's lack of information or restrained
by his being forced to discuss a remote topic. Second, the
validity of the technique is attested to by the greater variety
of linguistic structures expressed through interchange among
group members, as opposed to the one-child to one-adult situation described in free-speech sampling earlier in this
chapter. We would point out that *feedback* is also operating.
For example, in the usual method of gathering free-speech
data, the child says something to the adult and it is accepted
by the adult; if it were challenged, the adult would be guilty
of influencing the data being generated by the child and the
technique would be termed "invalid." In the peer group,
however, after a statement has been made, other group
members may challenge that statement, resulting in a restate-
ment, a contradiction, a hypothetical example for clarification, etc. What this does to the linguistic sample, then, is
expand the variety of linguistic structures to include cause
and effect, negation, subjunctive mood, etc., all of which are
seldom elicited through traditional free-speech sampling procedures.

Our initial concern of validity (the first portion of this
chapter), our interest in the *constructive* use of language (in
both comprehension and production) and in how materials
influence language generated, and a philosophical interest in
incorporating feedback principles into language assessment of
young children all led us to rethink the *products* and *processes* we were studying.

We began this particular research because of some interesting results we obtained as we explored methods to gather
some *process* data from an experimental preschool classroom.

We wanted samples of productions from the children themselves, which would show us how they were constructing their classroom experiences. Discounting the fact that none of these three- to four-year-olds could draw very well (something they were not so quick to discount for a while), we asked them to go in groups of three or four to small rooms apart from the classroom and to draw in a drawing book.

Procedure

We provided a topic for our drawing sessions, and we always avoided what might be termed a "static" target for the children to produce, for example, a car or a bus. In addition, our topics always focused on the children's common experiences. We were interested in how they *reconstructed* their experiences and how they might *transform* aspects of their environments. We were looking at *representational competence,* and by this we did not mean their drawing ability, but their knowledge that something with which they had had direct experience could be depicted graphically, in a two-dimensional space.

An example of a drawing topic might be a class field trip to a local apple farm or a nearby McDonald's. All children shared in the activity and the drawing topic was introduced by having the small group recall the field trip. A typical discussion that ensued, as in recounting the orchard, was for the children to recall machinery at the farm or things they did, such as riding out to the fields on a hay wagon. As the children engaged in their discussions, the adult conducting the drawing session gave the children their drawing books and asked them to draw something they remembered or wanted to draw about the orchard.

In some cases, the topics were more structured, to get the children to represent either familiar or new experiences. By asking them to draw themselves playing on the school playground, for example, we were attempting to elicit their topographical reconstructions of a familiar environment.

The responsibility for administering the task of drawing books is shared by two people, an examiner and an observer. The usual procedure is that each person takes a turn in each role with various groups. The groups should consist of three or four children.

The materials and equipment needed are a tape recorder and microphone, drawing books, and markers.

The role of the examiner is to hand out the drawing books and introduce the topic to the children. As the children draw they describe their drawings. The examiner writes labels, in pencil, directly onto the children's drawings. Ideally, the child will describe everything he has drawn without being asked, but if a child does not verbalize while he is drawing it is necessary for the examiner to elicit this information by subtly suggesting that the drawing is interesting or that she likes it very much. If that tack isn't successful, the examiner then directly asks what a specific line or shape is.

Each session should last about twenty minutes, but it is up to the discretion of the examiner to allow some children to take longer or to do more than one drawing.

The observer's responsibility is to start the tape recorder at the beginning of each session and to write down what is being said and by whom. Experience has taught us that writing down the name of the child and the first few words of each statement will simplify the task of transcribing the tapes because it is very difficult to identify voices when three children speak at once. It is also helpful for coding purposes to note, when possible, if the child's statements are elicited or unelicited.

After the drawing sessions have been completed, the observers transcribe their tapes. The transcripts of these tapes are typed and returned for later coding.

Classroom activities of the experimental preschool which we studied frequently concentrated on group discussions of topics such as "What is an idea?" "How do you know that you have an idea?" "Is your idea the same as someone else's?" Thus, it is easy to see that the children were used to thinking about nonpresent events and ideas and consequently they usually accepted the request for drawings about nonpresent events and experiences.

As the children drew, we looked for reconstructions of their nursery school experiences. To get the information, we asked them to identify various picture parts as they worked, labeling the attributes so we could code the pictures later. We were interested in the kinds of details children use as they recall events. It was interesting to observe that the children used their drawings more for communicative purposes if the adult who was with them as they drew had not shared the drawing topic experience.

We also used the drawings to check for memory. We had labeled the picture parts, and later interviewed the children about their drawings. Interestingly, one little boy did not seem conflicted about recounting the details from a black and white Xerox copy; he told his story again, ignoring the lack of color and the size discrepancy. No doubt he never thought that there could be two copies of his picture; the discrepancy was too great.

These were interesting findings, but they are not the primary data of the study. We found that the labels the children produce in their reconstructions as they draw reflect their cognitive organizations, and the *dialogue,* which is similar to the free-speech samples mentioned previously, can be evaluated for representational thought.

Verbal Reflections of Cognitive Organization

The categories of verbalization we attended to involve various aspects of representational thought. We were interested in the verbal behaviors of naming and describing for which it is necessary for the child to analyze part/whole relationships, location and spatial organization, and various qualitative features. We were interested in distinctions children make between ongoing (progressive) and habitual present-tense activities, descriptions that involve mental reconstruction in which the child has to search his memory to retrieve the critical attributes of events and experiences. We were interested in evaluative statements reflecting both positive and negative attitudes. Statements of intention, sequence, and planning reflect anticipatory representational thinking, categories also of interest. In sum, we wished to study children's language used for representing nonpresent events, past or anticipated situations, sequential and part/ whole relationships of behaviors or events, and hypothetical or nonexperienced *possible* situations. These categories reflect organization of knowledge. They also reflect the child's language knowledge because the child has to use language in a generative manner to convey his reconstructions or anticipations. Table 1 lists the classes of verbal behaviors we used in coding the children's stream of verbalizations during the drawing sessions.

These categories reflect the child's organization of his own experiences. The verbal expression of the organization does something else, however. These verbalizations objectify the experiences. The child can once again become an actor on an object of reconstruction or anticipation. Hence, explicit verbalizations allow the child to engage in objectified planning, sequencing, evaluation, and other commentary about a world that is known to him but is no longer physically present. The effect is feedback, where feedback serves as a reality check for reconstructions and as hypothesis testing for anticipations. The feedback is self-regulated.

We have been discussing autoregulatory processes that Piaget includes in his cybernetic model. Verbal behaviors, in this model, have been presented as a means for monitoring and controlling one's own actions, a use of language we see in language growth of three- to six-year-olds. The social-regulatory mechanisms are the other side of the regulation model. To study this aspect of the model we divided our analyses into two classifications: verbalizations about a child's own drawings, which we have already presented (Table 1), and verbalizations about peer drawings (Table 2). The categories for verbalizations about peer drawings parallel the coding scheme for his own drawings and, again, the feedback to the child is essentially self-directed. In this case, however, the self-directed feedback derives from what the child sees and verbalizes about other's reconstructions. Because the situation allows for interaction, the categories are expanded to include inquiries, comparisons, and helping (advice) statements. However, this aspect of the coding is only *half* of the picture of social-regulatory mechanisms. This is the *social comparison* component and it operates at the discretion of the individual child. The process is viewed primarily as an assimilation process.

TABLE 1

Verbalizations about OWN Drawing

Descriptive

    Naming
        part
        whole

    Describing appearance, location, or quality
        part
        whole

    Narrative -- progressive
        real
        fantasy

    Narrative -- past
        real
        fantasy

    Commenting on space

    Describing methods or ongoing actions

Evaluative

    Evaluative -- picture/product
        positive/neutral
        negative

    About ability/knowledge
        positive
        negative

    Request for help or information

Planning or Statements of Intention

    Planning -- What will draw

    Planning -- How will draw

    Statement of fact/appearance

    Planning -- progress or state of completion

TABLE 2

Verbalizations about PEER Drawing

Descriptive

Naming
part
whole

Describing appearance, location, or quality
part
whole

Describing method peer is using

Evaluative

Peer-evaluative -- picture/product
positive/neutral
negative

About ability
positive/neutral
negative

Inquiries About Peer Drawing

Seeks information

Notes discrepancy

Compares Peer Picture with Own

Giving Advice to Peer

Statement of Fact

The other half of the picture of social-regulation comes as a result of *interaction* among the participants. Verbal reactions to peer commentary and behavioral imitations, also expressed verbally, were coded in Table 3.

The feedback the child receives at this level is under the control of the social participants. The child is now in the position of having to justify or explain to others who are reacting to his reconstructions. Others are challenging his constructions for accuracy and for graphic organization. He can choose to ignore or to reject others' comments; he can justify or further elaborate his constructions for omissions which have been pointed out through peer inquiry; he may even modify his notions because of someone else's differing account of a shared experience. In this sense, the feedback serves an accommodative function.

The materials are the focus for feedback to the child, whether the feedback emanates from his own reactions to what he sees and comments on or whether it is elicited commentary from others. Feedback from the materials is very different from the picture or object feedback we discussed previously. Objects are not out of context or placed in contrived situations to generate a story context. Pictures are not confused by unnecessary complexities or interpretation of graphic conventions. The stimulus pictures here are an outgrowth of a meaningful situation that the child has chosen to represent in a way he remembers and in a sequence which is meaningful to him. The pictures are devoid of extraneous picture elements that we, as adults, are inclined to include to make the picture "attractive." Further, the pictures provide an opportunity for the children to interact around the so-called test materials because the subjects are generating their own test materials. There are four sources for feedback in this paradigm: (1) self-commentary about one's own work; (2) self-commentary about other's work (social comparison); (3) social interaction and reaction; and (4) feedback from the materials. Each of the other methods we have discussed provides one of these possibilities for feedback, but none is a comprehensive model, and that is why we have developed the procedure just described.

TABLE 3

Verbalizations Indicating Interaction

A. Reactions

   Reactions to peer comments

   Explains, justifies, or answers

   Agrees or repeats

   Rejects verbally (without justification/explanation)

   Ignores or doesn't hear (no verbal response)

   Changes label or aspect of story in response to peer comment

B. Influence

   Verbalizations indicating "borrowing" or other influence
      of peer drawing

      Borrowing of subject
         part
         whole

      Borrowing of technique
         color
         any aspect of technique except color

      Responds to peer verbalizations about peer's own picture

Conclusion

The study of early language development has proceeded along careful methodological lines. The data, however, frequently have been the products of decontextualized information, contrived episodes with strange materials, or misinterpreted pictured events. Hence, the methods for eliciting verbalizations we want to study are often the bogus element in evaluating children's language.

As children construct and reconstruct their worlds, they tell about their productions. Their drawings provide a vehicle for them to recount their experiences and, with a little prompting, the drawings facilitate verbalization. The technique presented in the discussion promises to be one of the most *valid* methods for gathering naturalistic speech data. Categories of representational thought appear to be equally meaningful as proper *units of measurement* for evaluating the speech protocols. We favor the pragmatic criterion in evaluating children's speech because it provides for both self-regulated and socially regulated feedback, serving the assimilation and accommodation processes of development.

References

Bellugi-Klima, U. 1971. Comprehension Test of Grammatical Structure. In C. S. Lavatelli, ed. *Language Training in Early Childhood Education.* Urbana: University of Illinois Press.

Berko, J. 1958. The Child's Learning of English Morphology. *Word* 14:150-177.

Brown, R. 1957. Linguistic Determinism and the Part of Speech. *Journal of Abnormal and Social Psychology* 55:1-5.

Brown, R. W. 1973. *A First Language.* Cambridge, Mass.: Harvard University Press.

Cazden, C. B. 1972. *Child Language and Education.* New York: Holt, Rinehart & Winston.

Chittenden, E. 1970. *Peabody Picture Vocabulary Test Response Analysis* (ETS Interim Report). Princeton, N.J.: Educational Testing Service.

Chomsky, C. 1969. *The Acquisition of Syntax in Children from 5-10.* Cambridge, Mass.: M.I.T. Press.

Cocking, R. R., and McHale, S. 1977. *A Comparative Study of the Use of Pictures and Objects in Assessing Children's Receptive and Productive Language* (RB 77-10). Princeton, N.J.: Educational Testing Service.

Cocking, R. R., and Potts, M. May 1974. *The Issue of Valid Limits-of-Measurement in Children's Language Productions.* Paper presented at the Minnesota Roundtable in Early Childhood Education. Minneapolis, Minn.

Cocking, R. R., and Potts, M. 1976. Social Facilitation of Language Acquisition: The Reversible Passive Construction. *Genetic Psychology Monographs* 94:249-340.

Deregowski, J. B., and Serpell, R. 1971. Performance on a Sorting Task: A Cross-Cultural Experiment. *International Journal of Psychology* 6, no. 2, pp. 273-281.

Gray, S., and Klaus, R. 1965. An Experimental Preschool Program for Culturally Deprived Children. *Child Development* 36:887-898.

Labov, W. 1970. The Study of Language in Its Social Context. *Studium Generale* 23:66-89.

Mackworth, N. H. 1972. *Verbal and Pictorial Comprehension by Children with Reading or Speech Disorders.* Paper presented at the 20th International Congress of Psychology, Tokyo.

McNeill, D. 1966. Developmental Psycholinguistics. In F. Smith and G. A. Miller, eds. *The Genesis of Language.* Cambridge, Mass.: M.I.T. Press, pp. 15-84.

Menyuk, P. 1971. *The Acquisition and Development of Language.* Englewood Cliffs, N.J.: Prentice-Hall.

Piaget, J. 1971. *Biology and Knowledge.* Chicago, Ill.: University of Chicago Press.

Potts, M. 1972. A Technique for Measuring Language Production in Three, Four, and Five Year Olds. *Proceedings of the 80th Annual Convention of the American Psychological Association* 9:11-13.

Reynell, J. 1969. *Reynell Developmental Language Scales.* Windsor, England: N.F.E.R. Publishing Co.

Shriner, T. H. Dec. 1967. A Review of Mean Length of

Response as a Measure of Expressive Language Development in Children. *Journal of Speech and Hearing Disorders.*

Sigel, I. E. 1975. The Search for Validity or the Evaluator's Nightmare. In R. A. Weinberg and S. G. Moore, eds. *Evaluation of Educational Programs for Young Children.* Washington, D.C.: The Child Development Associate Consortium, pp. 53-66.

Sigel, I. E., Anderson, L. M., and Shapiro, H. 1966. Categorization Behavior of Lower and Middle Class Negro Preschool Children: Differences in Dealing with Representation of Familiar Objects. *Journal of Negro Education* 35: 218-229.

Sigel, I.E., and McBane, B. 1967. Cognitive Competence and Level of Symbolization Among Five-Year-Old Children. In J. Hellmuth, ed. *The Disadvantaged Child* (Vol. 1) Seattle, Wash.: Special Child Publications of the Seattle Sequin School, pp. 433-453.

Wysocki, A. B., and Wysocki, A. C. 1969. Cultural Differences as Reflected in Wechsler-Bellevue Intelligence (WBII) Test. *Psychological Reports* 25:95-101.

7
A Cybernetic Approach to Assessment: A Problem-Solving Planning System

Mark N. Ozer

Introduction

A "disturbance" has occurred in the life of a child, a discrepancy between the perceived state of affairs and some reference state. Someone has sensed a discrepancy between what is going on in the development of the child and what is expected to go on. The reference state, in most situations, is a set of expectations for that child's development which are embodied in norms established for the particular age group. It is expected, for example, that all children will be using their native language by age three or four; that all children will learn to read at some level appropriate for their age and grade in school; that they will acquire some specific computational skills in mathematics at particular times. But this particular child is not matching norms for his age, and a disturbance is sensed by the child and/or the adults involved with the child.

The subsequent "diagnostic" assessment of the child with such learning or behavioral "problems" has traditionally been some sort of testing procedure. Such tests generally provide a more precise sampling of functions to document the areas and degree of deviation from norms—the areas and degree of disturbance. A determination is then made of the character of the problem in terms of established categories.

Problem categories now in use vary in their formulation. Some are based on a functional deficit, such as blindness, deafness, visual-perceptual deficits, auditory discrimination deficits, or motor impairment. These, of course, may be further subdivided into more specific descriptions. Other categories are more global and are based upon the degree of discrepancy the child shows from general norms for function. The various degrees of "mental retardation" are examples of more global categories. Thus, a child may be categorized as "educable" or "trainable."

Still other categories are based upon the degree of variation found in the areas of sampled function. The category of "learning disabilities," for example, is exemplified by an average score within the normal range on intelligence tests but with some subtest scores below the normal range. The total averaged score on the entire set of subtests may be in the normal range, but the child's scores on tests involving the language area below the normal range. It is this discrepancy between areas of function in a child with "normal intelligence" that is the basis for his assignment to this category.

Still other sorts of handicapping conditions are categorized on the basis of presumed causative factors. For example, those children considered to be "emotionally impaired" are selected on the basis of particular disturbances in interpersonal relationships, but they are assumed to have such difficulties to the "exclusion of intellectual, sensory, or health factors" (Rules and Regulations, *Federal Register*, 1977).

Once the "diagnosis" has been established by this testing and categorization procedure, treatment is planned. Such plans deal mainly with the goals that may be set for the child and with the administrative changes necessary to implement them. For example, plans might specify the need for special educational components for physical development, speech and language training, reading, and so forth. Decisions would also be made as to the appropriate site for obtaining special educational services. Children with greater needs might be assigned to special classes for the entire day, while others would be assigned for only a portion of the school day. Those still more severely handicapped might be assigned to special centers away from other children of the same age or might even be sent to residential centers outside their community. Evaluation would occur at specified intervals to determine the degree of accomplishment of the original educational plans. These plans would then be revised as necessary in terms of goals and the types of services required to meet those goals.

An extensive system now exists for dealing with children who appear to be failing to meet the criteria for their age. The number of such handicapped children has been variously calculated, but such assessment and planning activities go on in relation to a minimum of 3 percent of the entire school age population and, in many settings, 20 percent or more. A considerable amount of money, and the efforts of a large number of people are devoted to this system to insure more effective educational results through provision of more appropriate educational opportunities for these children.

In general terms, a sensed disturbance leads to activities to aid in planning for alleviating it, and a plan is then made, subject to subsequent modification on the basis of experience. It would appear that this process meets the requirements of a self-correcting or "cybernetic" system designed to bring about optimal functioning in the children identified as having problems. It is the purpose of this chapter to reconsider the assessment of children from a cybernetic viewpoint; to reconsider the products of such assessments—the data generated; to reconsider the process of such assessment—the way the data are generated; and to reconsider the organizational structure by which such assessments are done for entire populations. It will be suggested that greater awareness of basic cybernetic principles may make such an assessment system both more effective and more humane.

This chapter will first describe some of the issues and problems that the existing system presents to a cybernetic analysis, and then will suggest alternatives leading to solutions that derive from the theoretical ideas presented in earlier parts of this volume. The first step is to examine the existing system in greater detail.

Analysis of the Existing System

The existing assessment system will be considered in terms of its component parts: a sensing mechanism for the identification of children with problems, a data collection through diagnostic procedures, and an output product or educational plan. Each part will be separately considered, but it must be always understood that each is an aspect of the whole system and its underlying assumptions. These several components provide the context for an analysis which will focus the questions asked in this critique from a cybernetic viewpoint; e.g., what sort of data are being collected? How are these data being collected? What is the organizational structure in which data are being collected across populations?

Issues Concerning the Criteria
for the Identification of Children

Let us first examine a program for early identification of children with defects that has been carried out in a rural area in Kansas (Belleville and Green, 1971). The stated goals of that program are

1. to identify and correct all correctable physical defects,
2. to detect, and where possible, secure treatment for any developmental lags or emotional or behavior problems that might interfere with learning, and
3. to give teachers enough information to place a child properly in his classroom work.

One measure of the program's success is the degree to which those needing help are identified. Tests used for this would be selected to meet the general criteria of providing "consistency on repeated measurement, accuracy (true measurement), sensitivity (percent of true positives), and specificity (percent of true negatives)" (Meier, 1973). The Denver Developmental Screening Test is one that has met with widespread acceptance for simplicity of administration and good correlation with other already established measures to predict performance, such as standard intelligence tests. Considerable effort has been devoted to insuring that not too many children needing help are missed (false negatives) while not overidentifying (false positives) (Frankenburg et al., 1971).

Using a set of tests that met such specifications, the following results were obtained in the Kansas program:

- 10 percent of those screened on the Denver test were referred to physician or nurse;
- 11 percent of those screened for nutritional status and anemia were referred;
- 4 percent of those screened for hearing impairment were referred;
- 37 percent of those screened for speech proficiency were referred.

The population screened was relatively homogeneous, drawn from several rural counties of similar background. It is not clear how this population compared with the national norms that provided the cut-off points for referral. If one assumes that the population screened was large enough to show a normal distribution, then those with hearing problems appear to be under-referred and those with speech problems are apparently over-referred. How can we account for this? Was the reference point set too low or too high? And whose reference points are to be used? In operation, the decision criteria frequently change with the character of the population being sampled. If one samples children from homes poor in verbal skills, should the measurement criteria be those of their community or those of the examiner, who, in most instances, comes from a more advantaged community? This point is made because socioculturally appropriate norms are necessary for differing populations (Mercer, 1971).

The significance of proper choice of norms was underlined in a Special Project on the Classification of Exceptional Children in 1972 by the U.S. Department of Health, Education and Welfare. Particular concern was expressed because "large numbers of minority group children have been inaccurately classified as mentally retarded on the basis of inappropriate intelligence tests and placed in special classes or programs where stimulation and learning opportunities are inadequate" (Hobbs, 1975).

The screening instruments have mainly been designed for use by people who are not in day-do-day contact with the child. The tests frequently determine the existence of a problem independently of the perceptions of those who see the child on an ongoing basis and in comparison with his peers.

The design specifications for these procedures require the use of "objective," that is, independent, testers. The use of these independent measures sometimes inevitably lead to the improper identification of individuals who are functioning adequately in their real-life situations (false positives) as well as the failure to identify all those who need help (false negatives). Artifacts arising from the testing framework lead to such concepts as "overachievement" and "underachievement" when test results are compared with actual performance. These artifacts result from the assumption that an independent measurement process freed from the contamination of those who regularly work with the child, such as the parent or teacher, would have greater objectivity and therefore greater value. Petrie (in this volume) explores these assumptions and their fallacy in confusing the issues of subjectivity and bias. It appears that, in the name of objectivity, bias is not only not excluded but enshrined, as is evidenced by the need for a Special Project on Classification.

The identification of children with problems by those in daily contact may indeed be the more meaningful. One teacher, for example, may find that problems identified in the testing by an independent observer do not exist in her own interaction with the student. The teacher, either unconsciously or consciously, may have adapted the classroom situaton so that the problem is alleviated. Any test that identifies a child's "defects" may fail to identify the capabilities and/ or environment of the child that compensate or allow effective coping in spite of the "defects" elicited in the testing situation. Conversely, this same teacher may be unable to deal effectively with another child with a somewhat different set of characteristics. This latter child appears to be a problem to the teacher, even though the child was not so designated by the test procedures. The basic error is the underlying assumption that there is a defect that is independent of the context in which the child functions.

Still another characteristic of "objective" screening tests is the use of a limited set of tasks that would presumably show good correlation with the entire range of tasks in the real-life situation. Here again, artifacts arise from the testing procedure. The test items must inevitably sample only a limited range of functions, and the correlations must inevitably be less than unity in respect to the actual functions required in any particular setting. The fact that a child may have difficulty in a number of motor tasks in testing is frequently at variance with the fact that he is actually able to write; the finding on tests of a problem in "visual perception" is frequently at variance with the child's ability to read. Here again, the basic error is the assumption that the findings on a set of "objective" tasks somehow take precedence over the actual performance of the child in the tasks required in real life.

The proper identification of children needing more thorough "diagnostic" assessment may be met far more readily by means other than the extensive screening test system now in vogue. Using a longitudinal design involving pupils from kindergarten to fifth grade, Keogh and Smith (1970) reported that 90 percent of the pupils rated by kindergarten teachers on a reading readiness scale achieved in the predicted directions. Teachers rating children in their own classrooms in terms of the tasks used in their own classrooms were thus highly accurate in predicting the eventual outcome of children in tasks several years apart, namely "reading readiness" skills and reading. Other investigators (Ferenden et al., 1970) have found teachers to be 80 percent accurate in their predictions of learning problems in a sample of kindergarten children. It is not surprising that the finding of both difficulties and successes in the interaction of the child with the specific requirements of the school classroom could be a valid predictor of his future performance in subsequent classroom settings.

A Cybernetic Alternative

A screening procedure using teachers to sample the performance of a particular child in the context of their own interaction would be an appropriate alternative to an extensive independent screening system. This sampling would be in tasks relevant to a particular situation and would be on an ongoing basis. Such a sensing mechanism would involve questioning those in daily contact with the child as to their concerns. However, those in daily contact with the child, parent and/or teacher, would need training to become more adequate sensors. Fortunately, such training is a natural outcome of the very process of the diagnostician asking them about their concerns rather than asking it of himself in the context of the testing situation. With training, the question *"What are my concerns?"* can be asked increasingly by the direct-contact persons on their own. The process of specifying their concerns, followed by clarification in a dialogue with the diagnostician as part of an ongoing training program, woud result in fine-tuning the sensor.

Moreover, such training can make the sensing mechanism continuous rather than intermittent, as is the case in a one-time test by an independent observer. This is important since concerns may change from day to day or week to week. Another positive value is that the asking of the question implies the competence of the person being asked; it affords recognition of the individual as a control system capable of making decisions while simultaneously increasing such capability. It is the participant's ability to sense disturbances in such a dialogue with the diagnostician that is one of the products of the training. The training procedure will be illustrated later in this chapter in some case studies that show this sensing mechanism in action.

A cybernetic assessment system assumes that the individuals involved in any situation will attempt to deal with it to reduce disturbances. Individuals function as adaptive systems. In their daily life they are able to sense disturbances, and they may be brought to greater awareness of such capabilities. One aspect of child development would be the child's ability to sense disturbances for himself. A goal then in child development could be operationally described as the ability of the child eventually to ask himself whenever necessary, *"What are my concerns?"*

Issues Concerning the Diagnostic Assessment

Following the identification of children with problems, the existing assessment system leads to the classification of the problem for the purpose of administrative decisions, as outlined earlier. Various tests are now used to make an independent, "objective" delineation of the problem areas. I suggest that the questions being asked by those who carry out such diagnostic tests are those of medical diagnosis, regardless of the professional group to which the diagnostician belongs. The character of the questions, the data being sought, and the process by which such data are collected will be considered from a cybernetic point of view.

The decisions that are being made in the diagnostic process are initially to confirm the presence of "disease" as identified by the screening procedure. In medical diagnosis, the presence of a new heart murmur, swelling of the joints, and a history of streptococcal infection of the throat help the diagnostician decide that there is a "disease" present. Such a constellation of findings fulfill the requirements of "rheumatic fever." This medical model of assessment has been used to good purpose in the treatment of medical disease. A set of appropriate decisions flows from the categorizations made.

A similar sort of thinking has been transferred to the assessment of children with apparent problems in development. "Cerebral palsy" was the first of the developmental "diseases" defined. A category could be established like that of rheumatic fever. A particular constellation of symptoms and findings on examination help determine whether a child fits into that category.

A number of diseases are spelled out in diagnostic manuals. A disease must apparently be identified to qualify for treatment in the health system and for payments to be made for such treatment by various agencies in our country. This same principle has been transferred to educational treatment.

It is expected that the question as to the presence of "developmental disease" will be answered as "yes" or "no" in many cases. In still other cases, the determination of the presence of "disease" is a matter of degree and is made on statistical grounds. This mode of classification was exemplified by the establishment of the category of "mental retardation" and its various degrees. The individual may be described as "educable," "trainable," and so forth. Generally, individuals more than one or two standard deviations from the population norm are classified as abnormal. Although originally applied to intellect, the same standards have since been applied to a variety of functional areas defined by the norms of the particular culture, particularly in the area of "mental disease."

The presumption is that the categories established for the classification of developmental deviations are definitive. In fact, there are at least a dozen categories commonly applied to such problems. There is considerable variation even among the classifications different states in this country use to qualify a child for treatment. A child may qualify for services in one category in one state but not in another. The present classification system suggests only vaguely the kind of help a child may need, and "all too frequently, the labels lead nowhere or to treatments that compound the problem" (Hobbs, 1975). Indeed, the report of the Special Project on Classification goes on to state,

> They [the labels] are intended as much to protect society as to help children. Society in large measure defines what is exceptional, and to an indeterminate extent, labeling requires behavior appropriate to the label. Labels such as mental retardation or learning disability may provide teachers with an excuse for their failure to teach the child ... the label becomes a self-fulfilling prophecy.

In a recent study, teachers were shown a film of a "normal" fourth grade boy carrying out a set of activities. The first group of teachers observing the film was told that the child was normal while the second group was told that the child had "learning disabilities." The teachers then filled out an observational check-list used for the referral of children. Significantly more problem areas were identified by the teachers looking at the "learning disabled" child and significantly less academic achievement was noted (Foster et al., 1976).

The final report of the Special Project on Classification summarizes the present system of classification.

To call a child retarded, disturbed or delinquent reduces our attentiveness to changes in his development. To say he is visually impaired makes us unappreciative of how well he can see, and how he can be helped to see better. Federal, state, and local programs for exceptional children are organized categorically to provide a structure for legislation and administration, to encourage the flow of funds, and to increase accountability. Yet competent authorities agree that the categories impede program planning for individual children by erecting artificial boundaries, inhibiting decision making by people closest to the problem, discouraging early return of children to regular classrooms, harming children directly by labeling and stigmatizing, and denying service to children with multiple handicaps and to other children who do not fall into neat categories (Hobbs, 1975, pp. 15-16 passim).

The categories are thus both variable and at times arbitrary as well as inaccurate because the organism is seen as unchanging. The focus on the classification of disease does not lead to the determination of a specific plan for treatment other than in terms of administrative decisions. It is frequently ineffective even in achieving its stated purpose of administrative classification, and when it is effective in classification it is frequently harmful in its effects. It is also frequently inefficient in terms of the time spent and costs of professional staff. Energies are sequestered within this diagnostic procedure that could be better spent in actually treating the disturbances that are sensed.

A Cybernetic Alternative

The collection of data in an alternative system for diagnostic assessment would ask different questions from those asked in the diagnosis of disease. The question asked to begin to alleviate the disturbance sensed would be *"In your area of concern, what has the child been able to do successfully?"*

The diagnostician may ask this question of those who are in daily contact with the child, or of the child himself. Different data are being sought from those in the delineation of a disease. This question as to what has gone on successfully in the area of stated concern can bring about a change in per-

ception of those answering. It implies that there may indeed
be some things that are going well. It recognizes that the
child as well as those who are responsible for him are themselves functioning at some level of control even within the
area where such control has been felt to be lacking.

The statements by the person answering then confirm
what *is* rather than what *is not.* Confirmation—and a more
positive outlook—is provided for the person *answering* the
question by hearing about accomplishments in his own experience in day-to-day living with the child. The ability of the
person answering to sense the existence of his own control is
increased in the interaction with a diagnostician who en-
courages the stating of several instances of such success. (The
procedure for encouraging such statements will be illustrated
later in this chapter.) This sensing of success is a step in the
recognition of competence and is necessary for future
commitment in dealing with whatever disturbance may be
sensed. There is mutual recognition by the diagnostician and
the person answering the question that the latter exists as a
functioning adaptive system and does manage at times to deal
effectively with problems.

Ultimately, another goal in a child's development would be
his ability not only to sense disturbances but also to sense
when things are going well. Operationally, this second goal is
for the child to be able to ask himself on an ongoing basis,
"What do I feel good about?"

The diagnostic process in this new model has begun to
search for areas of health, of wellness, of accomplishment.
Different sorts of data are being sought. The process by
which such data are generated is crucial to the effectiveness
of the procedure. It is not the diagnostician who is critical to
the effectiveness, but the person who gives the answers. That
person must be able to recognize himself as having had successes even in those areas of stated concern.

In the standard diagnostic procedure, testing of the child
to determine areas of success is an independent function of
the professional diagnostician. In this cybernetic system,
quite a different approach is used. Instead of the parent,
teacher, or child being *told* what may be going well, he is

being *asked*. As MacKay (1969) has emphasized, quite a different message is being conveyed in an interaction by the use of questions rather than indicative statements. The grammatical *form* of the interaction has differential effects upon the originator and recipient of a message.

An indicative statement is intended to affect the state of the recipient's mind and subsequently that individual's actions. It is used to control the recipient. For example, the statement, "It is raining out" is expected to affect the recipient's state of mind and eventual behavior if and when he chooses to go outdoors. The effect is unilateral and directed to affecting the recipient. A question has a somewhat different impact since it has both an interrogative as well as an indicative effect. A question combines both an indication and an invitation for the recipient to modify the state of mind of the originator. "Is it raining out?" is an invitation for the recipient to fill in what is incomplete in the mind of the originator. It does indicate the area in which the recipient is to function while simultaneously inviting completion. It permits a bilateral activity or dialogue.

The questioning process initiated by the diagnostician in this alternative model thus invites the primary people in the child's life to express themselves. It permits them to describe whatever their concerns may be, whatever their successes may be. The invitation by the diagnostician permits them to hear themselves. The feedback loop within the person answering the questions is the crucial one. This process is even more important in relation to the next question in the collection of diagnostic data.

In the search for data of a diagnostic nature in standard procedures, the child is sampled in a number of areas to determine existing areas of both accomplishments and lack of accomplishment. The search is for present level of function that is then used as a predictor of future function. Data as to how such function may have come about and, moreover, how such function may be enhanced in the future are not collected in standard practice. Yet, it is just such data that would help those working with the child with learning problems determine *how* such problems may be solved.

The testing model in present use requires both the examiner and the person being examined to act with a minimum of interaction. The data sought are a measuring of the organism without inducing change. The goal of noninteraction is never realized in practice. It is, however, a constant ideal. The premise is that one is tapping an invariant system, unaffected by the process of measurement. As emphasized by von Glasersfeld in this volume, there is no way in which this can really be the case. Any examination must be an interaction between those involved. When that fact is recognized, it becomes possible to make the assessment procedure into a process that samples the conditions under which development may be enhanced.

More recently, the standard testing model has been modified into what has been called diagnostic teaching. The child is taught something and the examiner seeks to sample a number of options by which the child may learn a task or skill rather than just be tested for abilities already developed. The examiner teaches by varying the conditions of the presentation or the type and frequency of feedback on the results the child is achieving. In this model derived from operant conditioning, the examiner is the active agent in modifying the conditions (Bijou and Baer, 1963).

Although this model implies and actually samples the child's potential for change, it samples only the potential of the examiner for bringing about such change. That is, the performance of the child, when fed back to the examiner, serves to modify the examiner's behavior. It is the examiner who varies the conditions. The data derived from teaching the child are learned only by the person doing the teaching. What is being learned is what may bring about optimal performance in the child. However, the model derived from operant conditioning denies the child the experience of bringing about such conditions independently. The process of the examination in this model does not itself bring about a greater awareness on the part of the child as to what works.

There is a third mode of assessment, different from both the traditional testing model and the operant conditioning teaching mode. This new mode of assessment would sample the child as an adaptive system capable of alleviating disturbances—in this case learning something—and, in so doing, increase the child's awareness of how he has done so.

The interaction must become more mutual: the child learns about himself as the examiner learns about him. The new goal is for the child to become aware of the means by which a particular problem may be alleviated and the degree to which he, the child, can bring them into play. The products of the child's interaction with the examiner/teacher are the child's awareness of the degree of control that he took in the interaction and the means by which such control is brought about. The new question to be answered by the child as well as the examiner is *"What is working? What is helping to bring about the successes?"*

This additional question may be asked of those familiar with the child on a day-to-day basis. Ultimately, as with the questions about concerns and instances of successful alleviation of such concerns, the product of this question would be the ability of the child to ask it of himself. The search for diagnostic data in answer to this question may go on directly in the assessment situation and simultaneously sample the process of development while bringing about development.

This crucial question as to the means by which the child is able to bring about alleviation of a disturbance may be asked in the context of sampling just that process. For example, if the area of concern defined in the first question was specified as ability to read certain material, then it would be in that context that one would attempt to bring about some successful experiences to serve as the basis for answering this third question as to *how?* The content of the answers derived in a dialogue between the child and the examiner may then be internalized by the child as a means of control in other settings and for other disturbances.

The development of the child toward a more effective control system would, in my experience, come about more quickly by using explicit verbal instructions as the means of control. At first, the child may need to be informed by the observer about some means of control that may have appeared to be in use as they mutually observed some successful events (Ozer, 1977). The adult observer's role is to make these means of control the topic of discussion and to embody them as clearly as possible in instructions that may be used in the future by the child. The adult would seek the child's agreement or refusal to participate in the formulation. If the child agrees, the adult would ask him to verbalize the ideas that were offered. This verbalization step is crucial and is the basis for the child's using the ideas again in the future. In the next sequence, the child would have the opportunity now to instruct himself with the idea. For example, it may have been the opinion of the examiner that the child was able to read the material by looking at each letter and breaking the words into their component parts. If the child agrees with that idea, he is asked to verbalize it as a means of instructing himself in the future. In the next sequence, when the child is able to decipher the material, the question is asked once again: "What helped you do that? What worked?" Now the idea comes directly from the child. He verbalizes indepen-dently the idea that had perhaps originally come from the examiner. The means by which the problem was solved has become the focus of the interaction and may increasingly be used by the child in other settings.

It can be seen that the data derived from this diagnostic assessment are quite different from those ordinarily obtained. Unlike the testing model, the data deal with how the child learns rather than merely whether the child knows something or not at the time and conditions of testing. Also, unlike the operant conditioning teaching model, the ownership of data as to what worked is in the child. The product of the inter-action, initially, may be merely the transfer of some ideas as to some means of control from the examiner to the child. The development of a mutual dialogue about such means of control will ultimately free the child from the need for such dialogues and will start him searching for ideas that work. These ideas may be quite different from those initially offered by the adult. The child is learning to dip into his own "black box," as described by von Glasersfeld in this volume.

For example, a boy with severe problems in understanding and remembering what he initially hears learns to ask to have things repeated to him. He has learned that what works for him is to have something said more than once and perhaps given to him in shorter segments. He has been noted to be doing much better and no longer needs to ask for repetition as often. When he is asked what has been working, his reply is, "I have an imaginary tape recorder in my head. When people talk to me, I turn on the tape recorder and then play it back to myself." He had created a means to provide himself with some repetition of the message. That means for alleviating his difficulty is idiosyncratic and in his own words.

In the procedure to be described in greater detail later in this chapter, a further message could be conveyed by the dialogue with the examiner in reference to this question as to means. If, as described later, a search is instituted for *at least three ideas* in answer to the question, what the responder experiences is not only an awareness of some specific means of control but also that there are a number of such, whatever their content may be. Now it is the awareness of alternatives that is being modeled in the process of assessment. The diagnostic process, which now includes a search for some means by which the child may solve problems, is in itself a developmental process. Within the interaction, the number and degree of independent usage of the ideas may be seen to increase, and ultimately the degree of awareness that there are alternatives, regardless of their content.

In the design of a learning situation modeling this development of the child as a system capable of his own control, I have found it useful to specify the three types of feedback provided in the interaction by the examiner to the person being assessed. One is the standard feedback as to results, as provided in the operant conditioning model, and two are additional types of feedback.

The first of these two additional types of feedback concerns the means by which the results were obtained. I call this "informational" feedback because it is concerned with data that reduce the disorganization or entropy of the system. It is awareness of the means by which control was achieved that increases the degree to which the organism may

alleviate disturbances in a number of situations. It is the use
by the diagnostician of this additional type of feedback that
marks, in my opinion, the application of the cybernetic
principle of feedback to the problem of development, of
growth in adaptive ability. It makes the assessment itself a
developmental process.

A second additional type of feedback—feedback as to the
degree of control or participation—relates to the degree to
which those means of control are being provided by the child
in the interaction with the examiner. For example, what may
have been working for the child to learn to count may have
included the opportunity to hear the numbers repeated one
at a time, or not only to see the numbers but to write them,
or to have the opportunity to relate them to some rhyme, or
whatever. One may assume that the examiner had provided
the means by which the child was able to count "1,2,3,"
with the "agreement" of the child. By "agreement," I mean
that the child provided some sign of acceptance but had not
actually verbalized the means by which he learned to count.
At the completion of some aspect of the exercise, the child
would be told what had been accomplished in respect to
learning to count. The examiner would provide feedback as
to results and would also comment on the ideas that seemed
to work—informational feedback. The child would be told
what degree of control contributed to the use of that means,
that he had "agreed" to the idea.

The degree of control provided by the child in respect to
the ideas used in alleviating a problem may be roughly specified. I have chosen, in light of my goal of increased verbal
participation, to use degree of verbalization as one measure
of participation. The lowest level of contribution would be
acquiescence—non-resistance—to the idea offered by the
adult. That is, the child would "go along" with an idea, and
the degree of contribution to the interaction may be roughly
estimated as 20 percent. The child has been passive and
permitted the examiner to take the overwhelming responsibility. The next level of control is considered to be "agreement" in that there was some indication of commitment by a
nod or "yes." This level of contribution may be roughly

estimated as 40 percent. A 60 percent contribution would be a verbal statement confirming the idea that was agreed upon. Such a statement marks a change in the distribution of control, in that a verbal statement potentially available for use as an instruction had now come from the child. The preponderant control may be felt to be shifted to the child (80 percent) when he verbalizes from a "choice" of several alternatives. The adult has remained responsible for offering options, but it is the child who has had the freedom to make the choice and thus states it. The child answering the question "freely," without any choices offered, would mark a 100 percent contribution. The decision had arisen from the child independently at this highest level.

There is no attempt in this specification of degrees of control to obviate other ways of specifying the power relationship in any interaction. Such a continuum is merely offered as one way a situation may be operationally defined so as to provide explicit feedback regarding its nature. It is the principle of providing feedback as to this aspect of control that enhances the degree that such control may be exerted in other settings. It recognizes that there are alternatives in terms of degrees of control and seeks to increase such alternatives without suggesting that only the highest degrees of contribution are always desirable.

The quality of the means of control being verbalized may also be specified. One way of doing this is suggested by Powers (in this volume) in his hierarchy. For example, one level of statement would be "to listen." This idea would be at the level of "sensation" in Powers' model. A statement at the higher level of "transition" in his model would be "listening to the order in which to do it." At the "program" level in his hierarchy is a statement that the means of control is to "ask the question of what worked." The level of ideas generated by the participants in this diagnostic process, carried out over a number of occasions, varies with the individuals involved. Frequently, the ideas as to the means of control become those of the questions used in this planning process and the ability to plan for oneself—to ask the questions "What are my concerns? What has gone well in my area of concern? What worked?''

The development of the child is defined in this cybernetic model as a process in which there occurs increasing degrees of function as an adaptive self-regulating system, as evidenced by the ability of the child to become a sensor of his own disturbances, a sensor of those aspects of stability and equilibrium in the area of disturbance, and of the means of control by which he may have alleviated disturbance, not only for the present but for the future as well. As the process of collection of diagnostic data is shared with the organism being diagnosed in this questioning procedure, development is enhanced by the process of its sampling. Diagnosis is an episode of treatment; treatment is an ongoing process of diagnosis. Initiated by an interaction with the professional diagnostician, the procedure increasingly becomes self-initiated.

Application to the Issues of Classification

The data being collected in this alternative approach have been derived by encouraging the participants to come up with their concerns, their sense of accomplishment in their areas of concern, and their ideas as to the means by which those accomplishments came about. Questions have been asked rather than answers given. How can data derived in answer to these questions be used for the classification needed to place children in different settings in accordance with their varying needs? Classification may be based upon the *rate* at which a child learns. For example, one may determine the rate at which a child learns to count if that is one of the specific needs. The rate of learning, however, would be determined with respect to learning what is apparently at issue for him to learn; it would not be derived from measurement of what he had already learned, as indicated by some test of correlated skills, such as the traditional intelligence test. Measurement would be on tasks that have direct relevance to the child's ability to function in some real-life context.

Another criterion that may be of help in the proper placement of children would be the degree of independent control provided by the child in the interaction. Children who require considerable development in their ability to take an active role in their own learning would require a classroom with fewer children per teacher. Indeed, such needs are now a major determinant of a child's being placed in a special class. The difference is that the approach suggested in this chapter will generate such data.

Still another more functional parameter that would identify the child requiring special educational placement would be the number and clarity of the ideas the child is able to generate as to the means of learning. One may also assess the level of such means of control in terms of the degree of abstraction in Powers' hierarchical model. (See Chapter 2.)

No attempt has been made to be exhaustive in the description of the types of data generated by this approach that also meet administrative needs for classification. Rather it is suggested that the data translate more directly into degree of handicap and amount of resources needed to enhance the independent function of the child as a control system. An awareness of the principles of control systems permits this assessment process to sample such attributes better than the more static testing procedures presently being used.

Issues Concerning the Educational Plan

The output product of the existing system for assessment of children with developmental problems is an educational plan available for review at a later date, with subsequent modification in light of experience. The requirement for such a plan is itself a recent development. The passage of Federal Law 94-142 requires a written plan to be generated for each handicapped individual receiving special educational services, and at least annual review. Such an Individualized Educational Plan (IEP) is required by the Office of Health, Education and Welfare (HEW) to contain the following items (Rules and Regulations, 1977):

1. a statement of the child's present levels of educational performance;
2. a statement of annual goals, including short-term instructional objectives;

3. a statement of the specific special educational and related services to be provided to the child;
4. the projected dates for the initiation of such services and the anticipated duration of such services; and
5. appropriate objective criteria and evaluation procedures and schedules for determining, at least on an annual basis, whether short-term instructional objectives are being achieved.

Such written plans are an attempt, with appropriate safeguards for parental involvement and due process, to insure the least restrictive placement of the individual child. Some children may require full-time placement within a special educational setting while others may be able to function in less restrictive environments closer to the "mainstream" population. The thrust is toward the integration of handicapped individuals into the mainstream for both humanitarian and practical reasons. As indicated earlier, the Special Project on Classification recognized that the segregation of handicapped individuals served, inadvertently or otherwise, to limit the opportunities of those individuals. Individuals did begin to meet whatever expectations were held by those in daily contact with them. The label "mentally retarded," for example, limited the degree to which an individual was seen as able to function independently and the degree of independent function the individual actually evidenced.

The making of an individualized plan with specific short-term instructional objectives is also a salutary development. The requirement, similarly, for review and evaluation of such objectives also marks a degree of accountability that is relatively new and extremely important.

There are several issues, however, that must be considered in relation to the plans. The first is that high costs are incurred in making plans not actually carried out. The new requirements for plans have been grafted upon the existing system of testing. As has been suggested earlier, the data generated in usual testing situations do not readily lead to clear statements of goals that are truly reflective of the specific needs of the child. Goals determined by testers on the basis of independent sampling of the child frequently have no direct relevance to the sense of priorities of those in daily contact with the child or of the child himself. Rather, the question of goals should be asked of those who are in greatest daily contact with the child. It is their statement of goals and their resulting commitment that serves both to make such goals more related to the specific needs of the child and more likely to be implemented. Thus the question to be asked next is, *"What are your goals? What do you want to see happen?"*

When that question is asked in the context of what has been accomplished successfully, and how such accomplishments had come about, the likelihood is greater that the individual answering will see the future more clearly and with greater personal commitment. It is not only the existence of plans that is crucial, but also the process by which plans are made and who makes them that is crucial to their implementation. The regulations promulgated are but pious hope unless proper attention is paid to the context in which the plans are made.

A second issue in the analysis of the existing planning system is the need for a continuum of planning as well as for the continuum of services to be provided as a result of such planning. In actual experience, planning has been costly not only in the collection of data (not all of which is directly related to the making of a plan), but also in the expenditure of professional time in duplication of tests. The present planning procedures are so cumbersome that they have limited the availability of more highly trained and costly professional staff in providing direct services to children. Good planning procedures must establish priorities for the use of personnel and considerable simplification of procedures. The interdisciplinary nature of the planning procedures in most settings requires the collection of data about the child in a fragmented way wherein each professional discipline samples but one area of function. The high cost of the planning procedure also limits the frequency with which plans are made and revised.

The high costs of the planning procedures used at present thus have led to problems in the degree to which the plans made are clear statements of priorities, the degree to which the plans are complied with, the degree to which professional time is sequestered within the planning procedures outside of direct service, and the degree to which the plans made may be revised on an ongoing basis.

Issues Concerning the Revision of the Educational Plan

The primary goal of the assessment system has now changed toward the development of operational plans to be revised on a relatively frequent basis. One measure of the planning system envisaged by the Regulations promulgated by HEW is presumably the degree to which the goals set have been accomplished. It is not clear, however, what would be an appropriate measure. The goals set may have been far too grand, or more likely, quite inconsequential. How may one make the planning system itself be accountable for its activities? What criteria should be set for the degree of accomplishment of plans? One criterion would be to meet about 75 percent of one's goals. One may then have a considerable measure of success without simultaneously setting too limited goals. In other instances, it may be helpful in instituting a planning system that intial, modest goals be set and achieved in their entirety and that subsequent plans be more ambitious.

An additional measure of the effectiveness of the planning system may be derived. if the planning system includes provision not only for the measurement of the degree to which goals have been met but also resources generated. The modifications suggested for the process earlier in this chapter, as well as the sort of data that may be generated envisage the planning as a context for the development of resources in the form of ideas by which one has solved problems. In the context of successful experiences, the planning provides for a search for the means by which problems are solved. The ideas generated by such a search, involving those who are in daily contact with the child, are considered as resources. These ideas are the reflection of the resourcefulness of individuals in solving problems in relation to the handicapped child. Such resources are supplied by all the individuals involved, increasingly including the child. Thus, one additional measure of the success of a planning system is the degree to which it can document and elicit ideas that have been effective. Such data derived from a large number of individuals may well be an important source of ideas for the training of professionals as well as a resource for others with like handicaps.

Similarly, additional measures of the effectiveness of the planning system would be the degree to which participants are able to specify their concerns, describe those areas in which they have had success, their goals for the future, and so forth. One may measure the degree to which the participants are able to be sensors of their own needs and feelings. The final measure of an effective planning system is the ability of participants to carry out the planning procedures on their own. We have focused on the use of a series of simple questions, of a specified set of procedures to permit the ownership of the questions to come about as an intrinsic component of this alternative assessment system. A solution to the issues of the planning system would require such a highly specified planning system that may permit far wider diffusion of responsibility for planning—for each person to be ultimately responsible for himself. The next section of this chapter deals with the specification of such a planning system as it interacts with people.

Use of a Problem-Solving Planning System—A System Design

The planning system illustrated in Figure 1 reflects the ideas developed in this chapter. It is conceived as an expanding series of spirals. Growth occurs across time in the ability to plan in the context of making plans. The product is not only a plan but greater awareness of the ideas expressed in the process leading up to that plan, and ultimately the ability to plan for oneself, to ask the questions originally asked by the consultant professional. The function of the professional, regardless of the particular discipline, is to be a consultant, helping each individual participant take responsibility for the plans made, for the search for answers to each of the ques-

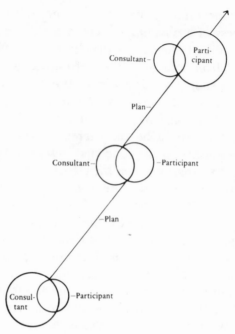

Figure 1. Degree of responsibility taken by participant in relation to that taken by consultant over time.

tions, and for asking the questions on his own. In each inter-action across time, the plans made may be expected to differ as will the concerns and the instances of successful experiences. Ideas about solutions may differ to a lesser degree since they may be expected to apply to a number of situations. What may be expected to increase is the degree to which the participant individuals are able to specify their answers to these same questions and to use the questions on their own.

Within each interaction between consultant(s) and planner(s), the entire planning procedure is carried out. At each instance, there is identification of a problem area, data collection, making of a plan, and review. The content of the planning sessions is based upon the use of the questions that have been developed in this chapter. The first question, concerns, represents the sensing procedure for identification of problem areas; the second question, successful experiences in the area of concern, begins the diagnostic process that emphasizes, in the third question, what worked in making such successes possible; the fourth question, goals, leads to the making of the plan. The plan itself contains the selected goals for the future and the ideas selected from what had worked in the past as the means of achieving the goal.

The steps used in answering these questions involve the participant in *exploring* a number of ideas before *selecting* those of the highest priority or some other criterion before then making such ideas more *specific*. In answer to each of the questions, at least three ideas are elicited in the exploration step. As I have emphasized earlier, the value of the search for three ideas is not only to clarify ideas; even more important, in my experience, has been the awareness by the participant that there are options regardless of the content of those options.

At each interaction, as illustrated in Figure 1, the respective circles represent the activities of the consultant (on the left) and the participants functioning as planners (on the right) in meeting the three goals of the planning system. The line running between the interactions represents the writing of a plan derived from the interface between the consultant and the client as the first goal. At each successive interaction to review the previous plan, the size of the circles represents the contribution made by each to the entire planning process, answering the planning questions. The size of the client's contribution increases in meeting the second goal. A third level goal is the progressive ownership by the primary participant of the planning procedure itself as represented by the arrow into the future independent of the consultant.

A unit of service in this planning system would be a planning cycle. Each planning cycle consists of answering each of the four questions leading to the fifth question on the plan for the future and its later review. The review is an evaluation of the progress of the plan and at least three statements of what was accomplished. The question then is what may have brought about such accomplishments. These two questions serve as a review both of the goals and the means, since the plan had contained both components. The planning process then is repeated.

The time required to carry out a single planning cycle may vary. In the example provided, the planning cycle was completed in a single session and another cycle leading to a plan to be evaluated in one week was started. The answers to the questions may be derived from memory or recent experiences of the participants. Or, the session itself may offer an opportunity to experience problems and solutions to problems such as taking responsibility, communication, or expressing feelings and ideas. Still another option, mentioned earlier in the chapter, is for the planning session to focus on specific concerns, develop some successful experiences and an awareness of how those were accomplished, such as in a reading problem or counting.

In this example of an interview first with a set of parents, and then with the parents and their son, the consultant asked the planning questions and encouraged the participants to take responsibility for their answers. It was the very process of the son's doing so in the planning that provided him and his parents with the experience of success in the area of concern.

A Sample Interview

The parents are interviewed about their son, a teen-aged college student. The first question relates to their concerns at the time of the interview.

C: *What are your concerns?*

P: He takes our car despite the fact that his insurance was cancelled. He is not taking his classes at junior college. He does not keep the agreements he makes with us, particularly about taking the car.

C: *What bothers you the most? What is the best statement you can make at this time as to what concerns you?*

P: The thing that bothers us the most is that he does not control his impulses. He acts without thinking of the consequences.

In the process of answering this first question, the parents explored their concerns and mentioned at least three concerns before selecting their greatest one. It may be noted that the idea selected in answer to the second question was somewhat different from those mentioned in the exploration step. It is that last statement that then becomes the basis for asking the next question.

C: *What has he done to "control his impulses"?*
P: He has gotten rides to school so that he does not use the car.
C: *How many times has he done so? During how many of the past weeks has he not used the car?*
P: He was responsible and did not use the car this past month.
C: *Then he acted in a responsible way this past week, the week before and the week before that. That is at least three weeks. Are there any other examples of his controlling his impulses?*
P: Now that we think of it, he did do something this past week that was really unusual. He did not go out with his friends when they called for him. He told them that he had to do some school work and wanted to get it finished.
C: *Which situation stands out in your mind as the best example of his controlling his impulses?*
P: That time when he told his friends that he wanted to get his school work done. That was really unusual for him.

The consultant has now helped the parents look at the times when the boy did what they had felt initially to be their area of concern. Their perception of the boy as not controlling his impulses had been partially transformed by recounting some situations in which he had done so. The consultant had made them see that the initial example they gave was a recurrent one that had occurred at least three times. In the context of such an exploration, the parents had come up with another situation that was far more positive. The last scene is now more specifically described in terms of time and place, in answer to a series of questions from the consultant. The attempt is made for the parents to relive that scene to answer the next question as to what may have brought it about.

In the next series of questions, dealing with the means by which the boy was able to control his impulses, the parents explored a number of ideas in a nonjudgmental way before selecting the idea that seemed to be most useful. In this case, the idea they selected was that "we told him, when he asked us what he should do, that it was his decision." What is crucial is not merely the idea that they came up with, but hearing themselves come up with ideas that may have worked. In interaction with the consultant, they had begun to look for ideas that may have general applicability, albeit derived from a specific situation in their own experience.

Their feelings of concern had been explored and then focused. They had begun to look at the boy in terms of some of his positive attributes, and to think about conditions that may have been effective. The past had been evoked as a context for planning for the future. That planning for the future then goes on in the next question as to goals. The next question is, *"What do you want to see happen?"* Again, at least three ideas are elicited before selecting the goal for the future. That goal was to "involve him in his own decision making," and the means would be the same they found had worked in the earlier situation. They would tell him that "it was his decision."

Since he was waiting outside the room where this activity had just gone on, it was possible to implement the plan immediately. He was asked whether he wished to come into the room and participate in planning himself. He agreed to do so and the process was now repeated with the boy as a participant along with the parents. The same questions were asked and he had the opportunity to come up with concerns of his own. The common concerns were then commented on by the consultant before there was sharing of the situations in which he had managed to do what was now their joint concern. There then was sharing of ideas as to what may have worked before making a plan for the future.

During the planning process, the boy took increasing responsibility for coming up with answers to the questions. The final plan included the boy's choosing goals. The plan was "to go to all my classes this next week" and the means, "leaving it to me and not checking up on me." The idea that had originally arisen when he had told his friends that he needed to do his schoolwork had thus been used again and again. It had been used in the planning process and was now to be used in the plan for school attendance.

In this particular case, a single one-hour session included the completion of one planning cycle with the involvement of the boy in planning for himself as the implementation of the parents' original plan. The degree of the boy's involvement may be evaluated by the number of his ideas and his participation in the planning process. Such participation was specified by the consultant at the end of the planning session as a means of making the accomplishment explicit. Another planning cycle would be completed at the follow-up in one week when the plan for school attendence would be recycled. The planning questions would be asked again and the answers as to concerns, successful experiences, and even what worked might be expected to be somewhat different. The goals for the next interim may also differ. At each interaction with the consultant, there would be feedback to the participants of the degree to which they were exploring alternatives, selecting, and specifying them in answer to each of the questions. The consultant maintains the structure of the planning process, which remains the same though the content of the answers may differ.

I suggest that what is being modeled in this planning system is the process of development. A third major outcome measure, in addition to making a plan and the steps in answering the questions, is the ownership of the questions themselves. The use of these questions as to concerns, what has been accomplished in the area of concern, what has worked, and what are the goals for the future is a structure by which individuals may evaluate themselves. The measure is the number of instances in which the individuals carry out such planning independently of the consultant. This is facilitated by providing the format for the planning on a printed sheet of paper for use by the participants. The role of the consultant at the time of review is to elicit from the participants concerns about the planning that they have carried out, what has gone well, and what has been the means by which things have gone well, before again asking them for their goals for themselves. The focus of the interaction with the consultant had shifts from their everyday concerns to the process they have acquired to deal with them. The focus has shifted to the technology used by the consultant and now being used by the participants. A clear, yet general, technology for solving problems has been transferred with various adaptations by the clients.

Development has been induced in the participants by their ownership of the technology. The entire planning system originally designed to deal with developmental problems has served to exemplify the developmental process it is trying to enhance. Planning reconceptualized in this way is an intrinsic part of the treatment. Assessment has become treatment and the treatment has come within the capability of the consumer of the planning services. To the degree that such planning is intrinsic to the day-to-day activities of the participants, they may become more independent as sensors of disturbances and successes in their lives, sensors of what works for them to alleviate disturbances, and sensors of their own goals for themselves.

A cybernetic analysis of the approach to planning for children with learning and behavioral problems requires recognition of the competence of individuals as control systems for themselves. It is the awareness of the issue of control that cybernetics highlights. It is the sharing of this control and responsibility for it that may lead cybernetics to provide the more humane use of human beings that was the hope of Wiener at the outset.

References

Belleville, M. and Green, P. B. 1971. Pre-school Multiphasic Screening Programs in Rural Kansas. Presented at the American Public Health Association Meeting, 13 October 1971.

Bijou, S. W. and Baer, D. M. 1963. Contributions from a Functional Analysis. In L. P. Lipsett and C. C. Spiker, eds. *Advances in Child Development.* New York: Academic Press, 1:211-231.

Ferenden, W. E. Jr., Jacobson, S., and Linden, N. J. 1970. Early Identification of Children with Learning Disabilities. *Journal of Learning Disabilities* 3:589-593.

Foster, G.F., Schmidt, C. R., and Sabatino, D. 1976. Teacher Expectations and the Label, Learning Disabilities. *Journal of Learning Disabilities* 9:111-114.

Frankenburg, W., et al. 1971. Validity of the Denver Developmental Screening Test. *Child Development* 42:475-485.

Gillespie, P. H., Miller, T. C., and Fiedler, V. D. 1975. Legislative Definitions of Learning Disabilities: Roadblock to Effective Service. *Journal of Learning Disabilities* 8:660-666.

Hobbs, N. 1975. *Futures of Children, Categories, Labels and Their Consequences.* Nashville, Tenn.: Vanderbilt Univ. Press.

Keogh, B. K., and Smith, C. E. 1970. Early Identification of Educationally High-Potential and High-Risk Children. *Journal of School Psychology* 8:285-290.

MacKay, D. 1969. The Informational Analysis of Questions and Commands. In *Information, Mechanism, and Meaning.* Cambridge, Mass.: M.I.T. Press.

Mercer, J. R. 1971. Institutionalized Anglocentrism: Labeling Mental Retardates in the Public Schools. In P. Orleans and W. Russell, Jr., eds. *Race, Change and Urban Society.* Urban Affairs Annual Review 5. Los Angeles: Sage Publications.

Meier, J. H. 1973. *Screening and Assessment of Young Children at Developmental Risk.* Washington, D.C.: President's Committee on Mental Retardation.

Ozer, M. N. 1977. The Interactive Assessment: A Means for Enhancing Development. *Journal of Creative Behavior* 11:67-72.

Rules and Regulations. Education of Handicapped Children: Implementation of Part B of the Education of the Handicapped Act. 1977. *Federal Register* 42:42478-42491.

The Contributors

Rodney R. Cocking is a research scientist with the Educational Testing Service. After receiving a Ph.D. in human development and family studies from Cornell University, he was a postdoctoral fellow at the University of Georgia. At present, Dr. Cocking is engaged in studies of feedback processes in preschoolers working on art projects, including monitoring the remarks they make while they work. His publications include books on cognition (*Cognitive Development from Childhood to Adolescence*, with I. E. Sigel) and language development (*Structure and Development in Child Language*, with M. Potts, P. Carlson, and C. Copple).

Howard B. Gallas is currently completing his doctorate in developmental psychology at Temple University and is senior research assistant in the Psychological Development Research Division at the Educational Testing Service. He is involved in a longitudinal study of the family and has participated in research programs assessing infant learning and adjustment, with particular reference to high-risk children.

Ernst von Glasersfeld teaches psychology at the University of Georgia. His main interests are cognition, language, and epistemology. For fifteen years after the end of World War II, he worked both as a journalist and as a research associate of the Center for Cybernetics in Milan, Italy. From 1963 to 1970, he directed a U.S.-sponsored project in computational linguistics. Subsequently, he designed the Yerkish language now being used by several chimpanzees at the Yerkes Primate Research Center in Atlanta. He is currently involved in research on children's development of number concepts.

Mark N. Ozer is a neurological physician whose work since 1964 has involved establishing assessment procedures for sampling the process of development and change in children with developmental problems. His interests extend from the use of these procedures in direct clinical practice with children, their families, and their teachers to the design of service delivery programs by which these procedures may be carried out on a large scale. He is at present associate professor of child health and development (research) at the George Washington University School of Medicine and associate professor of neurology (clinical) at the Howard University School of Medicine (Washington, D.C.). His publications include a book entitled *Planning/Assessment/Therapy: A Problem Solving Approach to Developmental Problems in Children.*

Hugh G. Petrie is professor of philosophy of education and associate vice-chancellor for academic affairs at the University of Illinois at Urbana–Champaign. In the latter capacity, he directs the program evaluation effort at the university. He has also written extensively in the areas of educational epistemology, philosophy of social science, and interdisciplinary inquiry.

William T. Powers has worked in medical physics and astronomy as a designer of electronic systems of many kinds. His interest in the application of control theory to living systems began in the early 1950s; he is the author of the recent book *Behavior: The Control of Perception.*

Irving E. Sigel is senior research psychologist and director of the Early Childhood Research Center at the Educational Testing Service. He received his Ph.D. at the University of Chicago. Since 1973, Dr. Sigel has been investigating social factors influencing the development of thinking in children. His theoretical orientation is exemplified in a recent book, *Cognitive Development from Childhood to Adolescence: A Constructivist Perspective* (with Rodney Cocking).